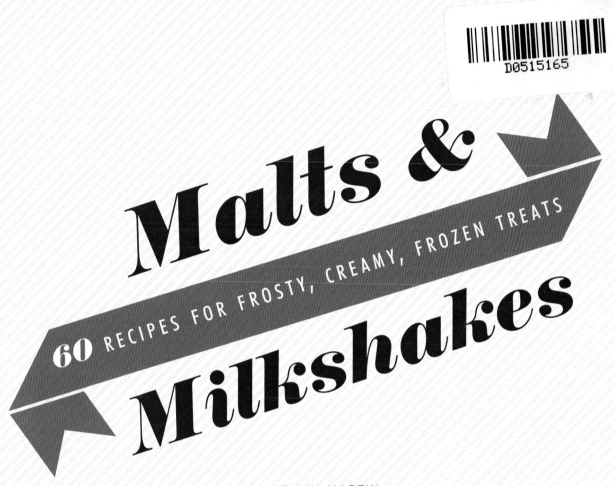

Malts &
Milkshakes

60 RECIPES FOR FROSTY, CREAMY, FROZEN TREATS

BY AUTUMN MARTIN

PHOTOGRAPHY BY CLARE BARBOZA

St. Martin's Griffin
New York

Copyright © 2013 by becker&mayer! LLC. Text © 2012 by Autumn Martin.
Photographs © 2013 by Clare Barboza. All rights reserved. Printed in China.
For information, address St. Martin's Press, 175 5th Avenue, New York, NY 10010.
www.stmartins.com

Food Stylist: Autumn Martin
Designer: Rosebud Eustace
Editor: Dana Youlin
Managing Editor: Michael del Rosario

Library of Congress Cataloging-in-Publication Data available upon request.
ISBN 13: 978-1-250-01464-1
First Edition: April 2013

10 9 8 7 6 5 4 3 2 1

Malts & Milkshakes is produced by becker&mayer!, Bellevue, Washington.
www.beckermayer.com

contents

thank you

It should be said that, without the recommendation from one dear, sweet Amy Pennington, I would not have had the amazing opportunity to write this book. Amy, you rock like none other.

Thank you to my editor at becker&mayer, Dana Youlin, for being so gracious and supportive during my first book.

Thank you to all the people and things from which my inspiration is drawn—I would be empty without you.

Mom, Dad, Brother, Sisters—I love you more than words can say. And thank you to Absalom Shantz, for giving me the most incredible, strong, and loving foundation a girl could hope for.

introduction

I love milkshakes: thick, velvety ice cream desserts with flavor possibilities that never seem to end. But milkshakes haven't always been the creamy, drinkable ice cream treats we have come to love today. In the early 1900s, drinking a milkshake meant sipping on spiked milk that had been flavored with syrup, usually strawberry, vanilla, or chocolate. Somewhere along the way, ice cream made its debut in the milkshake and stuck around (and boy, am I glad!). While the classic soda fountain flavors are still too good to forget, there are new milkshake recipes inspired from many savory and sweet creations that transcend the origins of the drink. This book will show you how to create both classics and modern interpretations by making your own syrups and flavorings. Good food, even milkshakes, always starts with good ingredients. For me, my entire "sweet" career has been built around sourcing the best ingredients to create the most extraordinary and delicious recipes.

After graduating from culinary school in 2002, by luck, fate, and some hard work, I landed a job as the pastry chef at the world-renowned Canlis restaurant. It was there that my knack for concocting imaginative, creative flavor profiles began to solidify into a career. After a couple of years, I became the head chocolatier of Theo Chocolate, where I continued to develop unique flavor combinations, including a line of ganache and caramel confections, as well as a line of flavored chocolate bars such as the award-winning Bread & Chocolate and Hazelnut Crunch. In a word, *fun*!

In 2008 I started my own company, Hot Cakes Confections. I created the Take-n-Bake Molten Chocolate Cake in a Mason jar, born from the classic dessert and reimagined here as a delicious milkshake. At Hot Cakes we take pride in developing high-quality, out-of-the-box recipes; this book also includes shakes featuring our Bacon–Oatmeal Raisin Cookies and our Smoked Chocolate, used in our famous S'mores cookie. Our signature organic Salted Caramel Sauce makes one of the tastiest milkshakes around—salty, smoky, and rich. A lot of the recipes found in this book can be used in other desserts as well. So be creative and explore: make enough caramel sauce for the shake but save some for your coffee. Or make a batch of our Salted Peanut Butter Cookies, use some in a shake, then make ice cream sandwiches with the rest!

I hope you enjoy making the milkshake recipes that follow as much as I enjoyed developing them. Creating sweet recipes is the passion of my life, so it was an honor and a blast to turn my kitchen into a milkshake playground. If it weren't for the crazy-talented chefs who came before and the countless people who inspire me, some of these knock-your-boots-off flavors wouldn't have come about. Thanks to those folks for showing the way.

Now go get your milkshake on!

appreciating your ingredients: they can make all the difference

In my career, I have learned the quality of ingredients plays a huge role in the success of a recipe. If you start with poor-quality ingredients, the end result of your dish will reflect that. So I believe in starting with the best; for me, that means local, organic, and/or responsibly grown and produced.

I am not a huge stickler when it comes to a certification, but I love to know the story behind the ingredients I use whenever possible. When you buy food that is fresh and in season, the flavor is so much more potent—it makes all the difference in your flavor profile! To that end, I am a fan of using whole, fresh fruit as opposed to fruit-flavored syrups and powders. Most manufactured syrups are corn syrup–based and contain artificial flavorings and colorings. This book strives to achieve the most intense flavors with the purest methods and ingredients.

ICE CREAM

There are two basic types of ice cream in the world: those made with eggs and those made without. A custard-based ice cream is made with eggs or just egg yolks. The other is made only with milk, cream, and sugar. Whichever style, there should be just four foundation ingredients: milk, cream, sugar, and sometimes eggs. Mass-produced ice cream has all sorts of other things added to it to keep costs down, textures smooth, and who knows what else. But I believe, the fewer ingredients, the better. You can make the shakes in this book with store-bought ice cream, or you can make your own using the recipes provided or your own favorite recipe.

FRUITS AND VEGETABLES

It is best to use produce that is in season and that has been picked when ripe. This produce has been allowed to ripen naturally and will have the highest concentration of delicious sugars, which provide a ton of flavor. If you can source your fruit and veggies close to home, that would be your best option. Unless of course you need mangoes and bananas, which are tropical and will most likely need to travel. Beware of frozen fruit that lacks any resemblance to fresh fruit. I have found that the flavor of frozen peaches, in particular, is difficult to match that of fresh peaches.

HERBS AND SPICES

The herb of a plant (in culinary speak) is its leaf and stem, while the spice comes from its seed, berry, root, and bark. I love including herbs and spices in my recipes, either whole or by way of infusions. There are so many roads to travel down using these amazing culinary transformatives. The saying "spice it up" didn't come from the clear blue sky: spices can create heat in a dish or enhance the flavors of a vegetable or fruit. They are also medicinal healers. Herbs and spices can be one of your best friends in the creative kitchen.

SUGAR

Ah, sugar. Sugar, sugar, sugar. I bet people were so elated when they discovered sugar! Lucky for us, sugar comes in many forms: cane sugar, maple syrup, honey, fruit, and rice syrup, to name a few. The most commonly used sugar—including in ice cream—comes from sugar cane. Sugar cane is grown in tropical regions and starts out as a juice, then makes its way down to a dry, crystalline form. In most of our recipes at Hot Cakes we use organic cane sugar, which tends to have a slightly larger crystal structure and a bit more residual molasses, meaning it isn't washed as much as "white" sugar, so it is actually a very light tan color.

Brown sugars come from cane as well but contain a lot more molasses than white sugar. In the traditional method of processing brown sugar, the cane simply isn't washed as many times, so a lot of the molasses stays in. Manufacturers can control the amount of molasses, thus making "light" or "dark" brown sugars. I prefer to use a dark brown sugar as it has more moisture and flavor than the lighter type.

DAIRY

Dairy plays a huge role in milkshakes. We use organic milk and cream from northern Washington State at Hot Cakes. The product is amazing—it comes from a single-farm operation, meaning they milk their cows and process and bottle all in the same place. Be sure to use milk and cream from cows that aren't fed antibiotics or growth hormones—these things aren't good for our bodies or theirs.

NONDAIRY MILKS

I know so many people who are allergic to dairy or are vegan and choose not to drink it. The fantastic news is that all of these shakes work great with nondairy ice creams and milks. For my shakes, I really like to use a combination of hemp and coconut milks—hemp milk is nutty, thick, and compliments the flavor of coconut nicely. But really, your choice of milk will do. I like to add malted barley powder to my nondairy shakes as a thickener. It also adds a lovely richness.

COFFEES AND TEAS

Perhaps you are a coffee drinker? Or maybe you prefer tea? And just maybe, you don't partake in either. Follow this simple rule when making a milkshake using either of these ingredients: if you wouldn't drink it alone, don't put it in your milkshake. Also, always use the correct temperature of water or milk when steeping, to avoid extracting undesirable bitter flavors.

equipment

ICE CREAM AND SORBET MAKERS

How important is it to make your own ice cream for these shakes? The answer totally depends on how much you like to be in the kitchen. If you love to make your own fresh ice cream, awesome—try these recipes and use them for these shakes. If you don't, store-bought ice cream will make lovely shakes as well.

Should you choose to make your own ice cream, there are many different kinds of machines to get the job done. I use the Cuisinart 2-quart machine, and it produces a fine ice cream. But maybe you like the old-fashioned method of the salt and ice hand-crank? Whatever method you choose, just remember to start out with a very cold ice cream base.

BLENDERS

There are many different ways to blend your shake. I chose to experiment with three different types.

The **classic countertop blender**: This guy is good for shakes with chunks to break up. Many of the recipes in this book contain ingredients that need to be broken down before the ice cream is added, and this blender does the trick.

The **milkshake blender**: I really love the texture of shakes made in a milkshake blender. Because its blades are not sharp or shaped like a blade, they don't "chop" or "slice" the ice cream but rather simply move it around really fast, causing it to break down. So the result is a creamier shake. But its downfall is that you can't pre-blend ingredients before adding the ice cream. So sometimes I would pre-blend with an immersion blender, then add the ice cream and finish with the milkshake blender.

The **handheld immersion blender**: This is one of the handiest tools in the kitchen. It is so convenient and turns out an excellent milkshake. It works much like a countertop blender, but you can move the blade around, which is nice. You could also make a giant milkshake in a 5-gallon bucket with an immersion blender if you wanted!

Which one is the best? Well, they're all pretty darn good. I love the versatility blade blenders offer—especially for chopping chunks—but I also love the texture a milkshake blender yields. If I had to choose one, it would be the blade blender. Whether you use a countertop version or a handheld immersion blender, it produces a lovely shake and you can usually find them at the thrift store for under $20!

quick tips for a perfect shake every time

You might be thinking, "C'mon, it can't be that hard to make a milkshake!" The truth is, it is not very hard at all if you have the basics down. I can honestly say that the first handful of milkshakes I made for this book just didn't have it. Once I discovered what "it" was, my shakes became exactly what I was looking for—creamy, thick, and fulfilling frozen drinks of goodness. Follow these tips for making amazing shakes:

1. Use soft ice cream. Place the ice cream on your counter for a good 5 to 10 minutes before you use it. The edges of the ice cream should begin to melt, and it should be easy to scoop from the container. This will prevent overmixing . . .

2. Don't overmix! This is such a crucial step. Overmixing results in a thin shake. Blend the ice cream into the milk until it is just combined.

3. Use your blender's "pulse" button. By pulsing, you can effectively break down the ice cream without overblending.

4. Use chilled glasses. Put your glasses in the freezer for 20 minutes before serving the shake—it makes all the difference!

5. Don't add too much milk. If you are a fan of thicker shakes, you can easily omit some of the milk called for in these recipes. When adding less milk, it is really important to make sure you are using soft ice cream.

6. Use quality ingredients. That goes without saying.

what you should know before you get shakin'

SCOOPS: The recipes in this book call for "scoops" of ice cream. My ice cream scoop measures 2 fluid ounces, which is a fairly common size. This means 8 scoops is 2 cups, or 1 pint, of ice cream. So whenever you see a recipe calling for 8 scoops of ice cream, know that it is exactly 1 pint. Easy!

MILK: I like to use whole milk. I find the extra fat yields a thicker and creamier shake.

MILK POWDER: Anytime I call for milk powder in a recipe, I am referring to nonfat milk powder. I love the Organic Valley brand.

SUGAR: I always use organic sugar, which is a bit darker than white sugar, from residual molasses. In turn, it has a deeper flavor than white sugar, and I suggest using it if you can. Otherwise, white sugar will do.

MALT POWDER: Anytime I call for malt powder in a recipe, I am referring to malted milk powder. You can find this at your local grocery store.

DOUBLING UP: If you are making a shake for one or two, please feel free to reduce the recipe. The recipes work well cut right in half. Or you can double it too if you want extra-large shakes or are serving a group. Just make sure you have enough room in your blender before doubling. Most counter blenders have a capacity of 4 to 6 cups, but if you are using an immersion blender and a large pitcher, you could make it all fit.

SERVING SIZES: Traditionally milkshakes are served in the classic soda fountain glass, which is 12 ounces. But really, that is a lot of ice cream to consume in one sitting. I think, especially if the shakes are rich enough, you can be satisfied with a little less. So most of the shakes in this book are meant to be served in 6-ounce juice glasses.

basic recipes

ICE CREAM RECIPES: *I am a fan of thick, rich, creamy textures. So I prefer ice creams made from custards. Custard ice creams are made with milk, sometimes cream, egg yolks, and sugar. The egg yolks help minimize the water content, thus creating fewer ice crystals, which in turn creates a creamier texture. The addition of milk powder also contributes to a creamy, thick texture.*

VANILLA ICE CREAM

CHOCOLATE ICE CREAM

GINGER ICE CREAM

VANILLA NONDAIRY
ICE CREAM

CHOCOLATE NONDAIRY
ICE CREAM

vanilla ice cream

INGREDIENTS

4 large egg yolks, at room temperature

1 cup sugar

3 tablespoons milk powder

1 teaspoon vanilla extract

½ teaspoon kosher salt

1 cup milk

2 cups heavy cream

Prep time: 1 day | Active time: 35 minutes

Makes about 1 pint plus 1 cup

INSTRUCTIONS

1. In a medium metal bowl, combine the egg yolks and sugar. Whisk the yolks until they are pale and fluffy, about 2 minutes.

2. Add the milk powder, vanilla, and salt, and mix until they are combined thoroughly.

3. In a medium saucepan, scald the milk by bringing it to a boil. Remove the pan from the heat. With whisk in hand, pour a little hot milk into the egg mixture. Whisk well. Pour in more milk and whisk after each addition until you have a smooth consistency.

4. Have your cream measured and ready to go.

5. Pour the custard into the saucepan and cook over medium-low heat, stirring constantly with a spoon. Cook until the mixture coats the back of the spoon, about 3 minutes. Remove the pan from the heat and immediately add the cream. Stir to combine, then using a fine mesh strainer (such as a chinoise), strain the custard into another clean bowl.

6. Refrigerate the mixture overnight, or you can do a "quick chill" in a shallow baking dish in the freezer. If using the freezer method, stir the custard every 10 minutes until the mixture is very cold and beginning to freeze slightly on the edges, about 1 hour. It is very important that the custard be evenly chilled and very cold.

7. Pour the cold custard into your ice cream maker. I use the Cuisinart 2-quart machine, and it takes about 30 to 35 minutes for the ice cream to freeze. Your time may vary slightly depending on what machine you use. You want your ice cream to freeze until it is thick enough to stand up on its own when you dip into it with a spoon. Imagine the consistency of soft-serve ice cream—it should be thick enough to hold peaks.

8. As soon as your ice cream is done, transfer it to a container with a lid and put it in the freezer immediately. I suggest letting it freeze overnight or for at least 6 hours.

LIGHTLY WHIPPED CREAM

Active time: 10 minutes

Makes ½ cup, or enough to top 4 shakes

INSTRUCTIONS

1. Make sure your cream is as cold as can be. In a small metal bowl, whisk the cream, sugar, and vanilla until soft peaks form. Use immediately.

INGREDIENTS

¼ cup heavy cream, chilled

1 teaspoon sugar (optional)

¼ teaspoon vanilla extract

note
You can use a stand-mixer or a hand-held mixer if you prefer.

chocolate ice cream

Prep time: 1 day | Active time: 35 minutes
Makes about 1 pint plus 1 cup

INGREDIENTS

4 large egg yolks, at
room temperature

1 cup sugar

3 tablespoons milk powder

¼ teaspoon kosher salt

1 cup milk

½ cup cocoa powder

2 cups heavy cream

INSTRUCTIONS

1. In a medium metal bowl, combine the egg yolks and sugar. Whisk the yolks until they are pale and fluffy, about 2 minutes. Add the milk powder and salt, and mix until they are combined thoroughly.

2. In a medium saucepan, scald the milk by bringing it to a boil. Remove the pan from the heat. Add the cocoa powder to the hot milk and whisk until smooth. With whisk in hand, pour a little hot chocolate milk into the egg mixture. Whisk well. Pour in more chocolate milk and whisk after each addition until you have a smooth consistency.

3. Have your cream measured and ready to go.

4. Pour the custard into the saucepan and cook over medium-low heat, stirring constantly with a spoon. Cook until the mixture coats the back of the spoon, about 3 minutes. Remove the pan from the heat and immediately add the cream. Stir to combine, then using a fine mesh strainer (such as chinoise), strain the custard into another clean bowl.

5. Refrigerate the mixture overnight, or you can do a "quick chill" in a shallow baking dish in the freezer. If using the freezer method, stir the custard every 10 minutes until the mixture is very cold and beginning to freeze slightly on the edges, about 1 hour. It is very important that the custard be evenly chilled and very cold.

6. Pour the cold custard into your ice cream maker. I use the Cuisinart 2-quart machine, and it takes about 30 to 35 minutes for the ice cream to freeze. Your time may vary slightly depending on what machine you use. You want your ice cream to freeze until it is thick enough to stand up on its own when you dip into it with a spoon. Imagine the consistency of soft-serve ice cream—it should be thick enough to hold peaks.

7. As soon as your ice cream is done, transfer it to a container with a lid and put it in the freezer immediately. I suggest letting it freeze overnight or for at least 6 hours.

on chocolate and cocoa powder

Not all chocolate is created equal. As with any crop, the tropical *Theobroma cacao* tree is subject to changes in different soil, climate, and growing practices, all of which can alter the flavor of the finished product: chocolate. Not to mention there are different varieties of cacao and fermenting and drying practices. Then, once in the factory, the way the cacao bean is manufactured can also affect the flavor. So you see, there are many ways in which one company's chocolate bar can taste completely different from another's.

The same goes for cocoa powder. Cocoa powder is simply the solids of the cacao bean, with most of the fat removed. Cacao beans may undergo one extra step before being pulverized into cocoa powder. This step is called Dutching. I'm sure you have heard of Dutch-process cocoa powder—the Dutching process is simply removing some of the acid responsible for bitter, sour, fruity, and tart flavors. This is done by soaking the cacao beans in an alkalized solution, which neutralizes the acid. Then the beans are dried, pressed, and pulverized into cocoa powder. Cacao beans that are not alkalized, or Dutched, are made into "natural" cocoa powder. Typically, the Dutched cocoa powders will taste more "chocolaty," as most of the other flavors inherent in chocolate have been removed. Natural cocoa powders have all of the flavor still intact, so the flavor will vary much more and could boast notes of red fruit, citrus, and other tart/acidic flavors. When you are making chocolate ice cream, be sure you find a cocoa powder that suits your tastes. There are many to choose from, both natural and Dutched, so have fun tasting!

For ice cream, I prefer to use a Dutched cocoa, which lends deep chocolate notes, reminiscent of chocolate pudding. Its pure chocolaty flavor also works best in our chocolate milkshakes.

ginger ice cream

Prep time: 1 day | Active time: 35 minutes

Makes about 1 pint plus 1 cup

INGREDIENTS

1 cup milk

3 tablespoons finely chopped fresh ginger

4 large egg yolks, at room temperature

1 cup sugar

3 tablespoons milk powder

1 teaspoon vanilla extract

½ teaspoon kosher salt

2 cups heavy cream

3 tablespoons finely chopped crystallized ginger

INSTRUCTIONS

1. In a small saucepan, warm the milk over medium heat. When it has just reached a simmer, remove the pan from the heat and add the ginger, stirring it into the milk and making sure all of it is submerged. Cover the pan with a tightly fitting lid or plastic wrap and let steep for 1 hour.

2. After the hour, using a fine mesh strainer (such as a chinoise) over a bowl, squeeze all of the milk from the ginger, either with your hands or using the back of a spoon. Return the infused milk back to the pan and warm it over low heat.

3. Meanwhile, in a medium metal bowl, combine the egg yolks and sugar. Whisk the yolks until they are pale and fluffy, about 2 minutes. Add the milk powder, vanilla, and salt, and mix until combined thoroughly.

4. Once the milk has come to just a simmer, remove the pan from the heat. With whisk in hand, pour a little hot milk into the egg mixture. Whisk well. Pour in more milk and whisk after each addition until you have a smooth consistency.

5. Have your cream measured and ready to go.

6. Pour the custard into the saucepan and cook over medium-low heat, stirring constantly with a spoon. Cook until the mixture coats the back of the spoon, about 3 minutes. Remove the pan from the heat and immediately add the

cream. Stir to combine, then using a fine mesh strainer (such as a chinoise), strain the custard into another clean bowl.

7. Refrigerate the mixture overnight, or you can do a "quick chill" in a shallow baking dish in the freezer. If using the freezer method, stir the custard every 10 minutes until the mixture is very cold and beginning to freeze slightly on the edges, about 1 hour. It is very important that the custard be evenly chilled and very cold.

8. Pour the cold custard into your ice cream maker. I use the Cuisinart 2-quart machine, and it takes about 30 to 35 minutes for the ice cream to freeze. Your time may vary slightly depending on what machine you use. You want your ice cream to freeze until it is thick enough to stand up on its own when you dip into it with a spoon. Imagine the consistency of soft-serve ice cream—it should be thick enough to hold peaks.

9. As soon as your ice cream is done, add the crystallized ginger and allow the ice cream maker to mix the ginger about. After it is evenly dispersed, transfer the ice cream to a container with a lid and put it in the freezer immediately. I suggest letting it freeze overnight or for at least 6 hours.

vanilla nondairy ice cream

Prep time: 1 day | Active time: 35 minutes

Makes about 1 pint plus 1 cup

INGREDIENTS

¼ cup sugar

¼ cup powdered barley malt

½ teaspoon tapioca starch

¼ teaspoon guar gum

¼ teaspoon xanthan gum

¼ teaspoon kosher salt

2 cups coconut milk

1 ½ cups hemp milk

½ cup rice syrup

2 ½ teaspoons vanilla extract

¼ cup canola oil

INSTRUCTIONS

1. In a small metal bowl, combine the sugar, barley malt, tapioca starch, guar gum, xanthan gum, and salt; set aside.

2. In a small saucepan, combine the coconut milk, hemp milk, rice syrup, and vanilla. Warm over low heat until the liquid is just heated through, then remove the pan from the heat. Pour a little bit of the warm liquid into the bowl with the powders, whisking as you pour. Create a thin paste by adding more liquid and whisking continually. Add your paste to the pot of warm liquid and whisk well.

3. Return the pan to the stove and, whisking continually, bring the liquid to a simmer. Remove the pan from the heat again and whisk in the canola oil. Strain if needed.

4. Refrigerate the mixture overnight, or you can do a "quick chill" in a shallow baking dish in the freezer. If using the freezer method, stir the ice cream base every 10 minutes until the mixture is very cold and beginning to freeze slightly on the edges, about 1 hour. It is very important that the ice cream base be evenly chilled and very cold.

5. Pour the cold ice cream base into your ice cream maker. I use the Cuisinart 2-quart machine, and it takes about 30 to 35 minutes for the ice cream to freeze. Your time may vary slightly depending on what machine you use. You want your ice cream to freeze until it is thick enough to stand up on its own when you dip into it with a spoon. Imagine the consistency of soft-serve ice cream—it should be thick enough to hold peaks.

6. As soon as your ice cream is done, transfer it to a container with a lid and put it in the freezer immediately. I suggest letting it freeze overnight or for at least 6 hours.

note

You can find guar gum, xanthan gum, tapioca starch, and rice syrup at health food stores or online. I have only been able to find powdered barley malt online: GloryBee Foods (www. glorybeefoods.com) is a great source.

chocolate nondairy ice cream

INGREDIENTS

¼ cup sugar

¼ cup powdered barley malt

½ teaspoon tapioca starch

¼ teaspoon guar gum

¼ teaspoon xanthan gum

¼ teaspoon salt

2 cups coconut milk

1½ cups hemp milk

½ cup cocoa powder

½ cup rice syrup

2½ teaspoons vanilla extract

¼ cup canola oil

Prep time: 1 day | Active time: 35 minutes

Makes about 1 pint plus 1 cup

INSTRUCTIONS

1. In a small metal bowl, combine the sugar, barley malt, tapioca starch, guar gum, xanthan gum, and salt; set aside.

2. In a small saucepan, combine the coconut milk, hemp milk, cocoa powder, rice syrup, and vanilla. Whisk until the cocoa powder is incorporated. Warm over low heat until the liquid is just heated through, then remove the pan from the heat. Pour a little bit of the warm liquid into the bowl with the powders, whisking as you pour. Create a thin paste by adding more liquid and whisking continually. Add your paste to the pot of warm liquid and whisk well.

3. Return the pan to the stove and, whisking continually, bring the liquid to a simmer. Remove the pan from the heat again and whisk in the canola oil.

4. Refrigerate the mixture overnight, or you can do a "quick chill" in a shallow baking dish in the freezer. If using the freezer method, stir the ice cream base every 10 minutes until the mixture is very cold and beginning to freeze slightly on the edges, about 1 hour. It is very important that the ice cream base be evenly chilled and very cold.

5. Pour the cold ice cream base into your ice cream maker. I use the Cuisinart 2-quart machine, and it takes about 30 to 35 minutes for the ice cream to freeze. Your time may vary slightly depending on what machine you use. You want your ice cream to freeze until it is thick enough to stand up on its own when you dip into it with a spoon. Imagine the consistency of soft-serve ice cream—it should be thick enough to hold peaks.

6. As soon as your ice cream is done, transfer it to a container with a lid and put it in the freezer immediately. I suggest letting it freeze overnight or for at least 6 hours.

note
For a fun version of this treat, stir cookie crumbles in at the end before freezing.

soda fountain classics

VANILLA BEAN SHAKE
OR MALT

BANANA SHAKE

STRAWBERRY SHAKE

COCONUT SHAKE

BUTTERSCOTCH
SHAKE OR MALT

ESPRESSO SHAKE

DARK CHOCOLATE SHAKE
OR MALT

MILK CHOCOLATE SHAKE

PEANUT BUTTER SHAKE

FRESH MINT SHAKE

EGGNOG SHAKE

SWEET CREAM AND
COOKIES SHAKE

THE BLACKSTRAP SHAKE

SALTED MALTED MALT

PASSION FRUIT
CREAMSICLE SHAKE

vanilla bean shake or malt

Although widely used as a staple flavor, vanilla is actually one of the most exotic spices available. It is the stamen of a beautiful orchid, and it couldn't be more unique! This shake is one of those classics that dates back to a time before ice cream was involved with milkshakes. In order to boost the vanilla flavor as much as possible, I use both the vanilla pod and its seeds, as well as vanilla extract.

Prep time: 1 hour | Active time: 15 minutes
Serves 4 in 6-ounce glasses

INGREDIENTS

¾ cup milk

2 vanilla beans

2 tablespoons milk powder

2 tablespoons sugar

1 tablespoon plus 1 teaspoon vanilla extract

Pinch of kosher salt

8 scoops Vanilla Ice Cream (page 16) or store-bought

note
This recipe is delicious as a malt! Add 2 tablespoons of malt powder along with the milk powder to the infused milk.

INSTRUCTIONS

1. In a small saucepan, gently warm the milk over medium heat. With a knife, split the vanilla beans lengthwise and scrape the seeds into the milk, then add the pods, making sure both pods and seeds are fully submerged. Once the milk comes to a simmer, remove the pan from the heat.

2. Cover it with a tightly fitting lid or plastic wrap and let the vanilla steep for 1 hour.

3. Remove the pods from the milk and discard. Blend the infused milk, milk powder, sugar, vanilla, and salt until they are nice and smooth. Add the ice cream and blend until it is mostly incorporated.

4. Pour into glasses and enjoy!

banana shake

Growing up, my favorite Popsicle was the banana-flavored Twin Pop. If it weren't for the artificial flavor and coloring, I might still be eating them more than just in the occasional nostalgic moment.

This Banana Shake is an homage to my childhood favorite without all the artificial ingredients. It truly is transformed by the addition of the milk powder, which gives the shake a richer, creamier texture and body. The salt is essential as it helps bring out the banana flavor.

Active time: 10 minutes
Serves 4 in 6-ounce glasses

INSTRUCTIONS

1. Blend the bananas, milk, sugar, milk powder, and salt until nice and smooth. Add the ice cream and blend until it is just incorporated.

2. Pour into glasses and enjoy!

INGREDIENTS

2 large ripe bananas

1 cup milk

2 tablespoons sugar

$\frac{1}{2}$ cup milk powder

Generous pinch of kosher salt

8 scoops Vanilla Ice Cream (page 16) or store-bought

note
If you also loved those banana Twin Pops, try blending one into your shake. It will take you back!

strawberry shake

INGREDIENTS

1 cup Strawberry Syrup (recipe follows), plus more for garnish

$\frac{1}{2}$ cup milk

1 tablespoon milk powder

8 scoops Vanilla Ice Cream (page 16) or store-bought, or strawberry ice cream

There may not be anything better than fresh strawberries from the garden—except maybe taking those fresh strawberries and turning them into a delectable milkshake! In keeping with traditional soda fountain methods, this Strawberry Shake uses a syrup made from either fresh or frozen berries—both are delicious. The syrup concentrates the strawberry flavor so you can make a shake without it turning into a smoothie. Using strawberry ice cream instead of vanilla is delicious and adds twice the flavor! Just be sure to choose a strawberry ice cream that doesn't contain artificial flavoring.

Prep time: 45 minutes | Active time: 5 minutes
Serves 4 in 6-ounce glasses

INSTRUCTIONS

1. Blend the milk and milk powder until smooth. Add the strawberry syrup and ice cream and blend until the ice cream is just incorporated.

2. Pour into glasses and garnish with a drizzle of the strawberry syrup.

note
If you like your shake with hunks of strawberry, pull the berries from the syrup before blending and stir them in afterward.

INGREDIENTS

2 cups chopped strawberries, fresh or frozen

¾ cup sugar

Squeeze of lemon

STRAWBERRY SYRUP

This bright strawberry syrup tastes of summer's delicious offerings. Be sure not to overcook as it will turn dark and begin to take on a molasses flavor, losing its fresh brightness.

Makes 1¼ cups

INSTRUCTIONS

1. In a small saucepan, cook the strawberries, sugar, and lemon juice over medium heat, until the sugar has dissolved and the mixture comes to a simmer. You may need to mash up the berries in order for them to release their juice.

2. Simmer for 2 more minutes, then remove the pan from the heat and allow the syrup to cool.

tip

Leftover strawberry syrup will keep, refrigerated, for 2 weeks. Try it on a sundae, or add it to sparkling mineral water for a bright homemade soda!

coconut shake

Sadly, artificial coconut flavorings have marred our perception of what coconut really tastes like. This shake strives to fix that. Instead of a coconut-flavored syrup, I use coconut cream in both liquid and powder forms to create a milkshake that tastes pretty darn close to the real thing. Coconut cream powder can be found in most Asian supermarkets or specialty stores.

If you want to get fancy-pants, scrape the meat of a small young coconut into this shake before blending. If you want to get even fancier, add some toasted coconut flakes and curry powder. I promise it tastes better than it sounds!

You can use coconut sorbet or Nondairy Vanilla Ice Cream (page 24) in lieu of ice cream to make this shake nondairy.

Active time: 10 minutes
Serves 4 in 6-ounce glasses

INGREDIENTS

1 cup coconut cream

¾ cup coconut cream powder

2 tablespoons sugar

Pinch of kosher salt

8 scoops Vanilla Ice Cream (page 16) or store-bought

2 tablespoons finely shredded unsweetened coconut flakes, toasted (optional), plus more for garnish

2 teaspoons curry powder (optional)

INSTRUCTIONS

1. Blend the coconut cream, coconut cream powder, sugar, and salt until nice and smooth. Add the ice cream, toasted coconut, and curry powder (if using), and blend until the ice cream is just incorporated.

2. Pour into glasses and garnish with toasted coconut.

tip
To toast coconut, use the smallest unsweetened flakes you can find. Warm a cast-iron skillet or sauté pan over medium heat. Add the shredded coconut, stirring constantly to ensure even browning, and cook until it is golden brown. Transfer the coconut to a plate and allow it to cool before using.

butterscotch shake or malt

When I used to think of butterscotch, those butterscotch chips you can buy next to the chocolate chips in the grocery store would immediately come to mind. It wasn't until just recently, when I had the pleasure of tasting real butterscotch, that I discovered it couldn't be more different than the store-bought version and is so much better. It's a simple thing to make and tastes like a cozy winter night next to the fire. Consider doubling the butterscotch sauce recipe and keeping some in the fridge for an ice cream topping or a delicious hot drink mix (just add to hot milk!).

Prep time: 30 minutes | Active time: 5 minutes
Serves 4 in 6-ounce glasses

INGREDIENTS

$1\frac{1}{2}$ sticks unsalted butter

$1\frac{1}{2}$ cups heavy cream

$1\frac{1}{2}$ cups dark brown sugar, packed, plus more for garnish

$1\frac{1}{2}$ teaspoons vanilla extract

$\frac{3}{4}$ teaspoon kosher salt

10 scoops Vanilla Ice Cream (page 16) or store-bought

INSTRUCTIONS

1. To make the butterscotch sauce: Melt the butter in a small saucepan over medium heat. Add the cream, brown sugar, vanilla, and salt, and stir until they are thoroughly combined.

2. Bring the sauce to a boil and continue stirring for about 4 minutes, or until it becomes thicker, and the color and flavor have deepened (blow on your spoon to cool before tasting, as this sauce is *hot*!). Remove the pan from the heat and allow the sauce to cool completely.

3. Blend the butterscotch sauce and ice cream until they are just combined.

4. Pour into glasses and garnish with a sprinkling of brown sugar.

note
This recipe is delicious as a malt! Add 2 tablespoons malt powder to the butterscotch and ice cream before blending.

espresso shake

INGREDIENTS

¾ cup espresso or very strong
brewed coffee, chilled

2 tablespoons milk powder

Pinch of kosher salt

8 scoops Vanilla Ice Cream
(page 16) or store-bought

To make this milkshake right, there are two very important steps: first, you must use the highest-quality coffee available to you. I have my favorites here in Seattle, and they range from medium to dark roasts. Whatever origin or roast you are into right now, use it. Second, you will need to make some form of espresso or very strong, concentrated coffee. I like to use a stovetop Italian espresso maker. If you are using a French press, grind the beans a bit finer than normal (somewhere between drip and espresso) and use three times the normal amount to make a really strong brew. Following these two steps will ensure a flavorful espresso milkshake.

Prep time: 30 minutes | Active time: 5 minutes
Serves 4 in 6-ounce glasses

INSTRUCTIONS

1. Blend the espresso, milk powder, and salt until nice and smooth. Add the ice cream and blend until it is just incorporated.

2. Pour into glasses and enjoy!

note
If you like the texture, you can throw in some whole beans for added crunch and coffee strength!

dark chocolate shake or malt

For those who enjoy their dessert on the less sweet side, this milkshake is for you. The addition of cocoa powder boosts the chocolate flavor without adding any extra sugar. The pinch of salt in this recipe makes such a big difference—it enhances the flavor of the chocolate, so don't skip it!

Active time: 5 minutes
Serves 4 in 6-ounce glasses

INSTRUCTIONS

1. Blend the milk, cocoa powder, and salt until nice and smooth. Add the ice cream and blend until it is just incorporated.

2. Pour into glasses and garnish with a dollop of whipped cream and a dusting of cocoa powder.

INGREDIENTS

½ cup milk

½ cup cocoa powder, plus more for garnish

Pinch of kosher salt

8 scoops Chocolate Ice Cream (page 18) or store-bought

1 recipe unsweetened Lightly Whipped Cream (page 17), for garnish

note
This recipe is delicious as a malt! Just add 2 tablespoons of malted milk powder to the milk and cocoa powder.

milk chocolate shake

1 cup milk

½ cup milk powder

2 tablespoons sugar

10 scoops Chocolate Ice Cream
(page 18) or store-bought

1 recipe unsweetened Lightly
Whipped Cream (page 17),
for garnish

Cocoa powder, for garnish

I have always been a fan of super creamy textures, but I can't stand cloyingly sweet milk chocolate—so finding a milk chocolate that was both creamy but not too sweet was a challenge. Until Theo Chocolate came along. Theo makes the best milk chocolate I have ever tasted—nice and dark and very creamy, with notes of caramel—yum!

Milk chocolate is made from cocoa solids with the addition of sugar and milk powder. This Milk Chocolate Shake uses a similar approach to that of a chocolate factory, but using ice cream instead of cocoa mass. The addition of the milk powder is crucial to achieve milk-chocolaty results.

Active time: 5 minutes
Serves 4 in 6-ounce glasses

INSTRUCTIONS

1. Blend the milk, milk powder, and sugar until smooth and frothy. Add the ice cream and blend until it is just incorporated.

2. Pour into glasses and garnish with whipped cream and a dusting of cocoa powder.

peanut butter shake

This Peanut Butter Shake happens to be in the top three of my favorites. I have plumped up the peanut butter goodness with the addition of our cookie chunks and little sparkles of candied peanuts. If you are a fan of a smoother shake, you don't have to add the extras. But I urge you to make the cookies—at least for nibbling, if not for ice cream sandwiches.

Prep time: 1 hour | Active time: 15 minutes
Serves 4 in 6-ounce glasses

INSTRUCTIONS

1. To make the candied peanuts: Combine the peanuts and sugar in the bowl of a food processor and pulse until the nuts are finely chopped. Be sure not to grind too much or you will make peanut butter!

2. In a small sauté pan over medium heat, warm the candied peanuts, stirring constantly. After about 1 minute, the sugar will begin to melt, so be sure to keep stirring at this point. Cook, stirring, for another minute, or until the nuts are light brown and the sugar has melted.

3. Immediately transfer the candied peanuts to a plate and allow to cool.

4. To make the shake: Blend the peanut butter, sugar, milk, and salt until nice and smooth. Add the ice cream and blend until it is just incorporated. (This shake is thick, so you may need to scrape down the sides of the blender.)

5. Stir in 2 tablespoons of the candied peanuts and the cookie chunks.

6. Pour into glasses and garnish with a sprinkling of candied peanuts. You may want to eat this shake with a spoon!

INGREDIENTS

CANDIED PEANUTS

$\frac{1}{4}$ cup unroasted peanuts

2 tablespoons sugar

SHAKE

$1\frac{1}{2}$ cups natural salted creamy peanut butter

2 tablespoons sugar

$\frac{1}{2}$ cup milk

Pinch of kosher salt

8 scoops Vanilla Ice Cream (page 16) or store-bought

$\frac{3}{4}$ cup Salted Peanut Butter Cookie chunks (recipe follows)

INGREDIENTS

2 cups plus 1 teaspoon all-purpose or pastry flour

1 teaspoon baking soda

1 tablespoon plus 1 teaspoon kosher salt

2 sticks plus $3\frac{1}{2}$ tablespoons unsalted butter, at room temperature

$1\frac{1}{4}$ cups dark brown sugar, packed

$\frac{3}{4}$ cup plus $2\frac{1}{2}$ tablespoons sugar

2 large eggs

$1\frac{1}{2}$ cups natural salted creamy peanut butter

2 teaspoons vanilla extract

SALTED PEANUT BUTTER COOKIES

Peanut butter cookies are my favorite. I wanted to develop a cookie that was moist, super peanut-buttery and that was a little out of the ordinary. This recipe fits the bill. The addition of salt takes this cookie to a whole new level.

Makes about 20 four-inch cookies

INSTRUCTIONS

1. Preheat the oven to 350 degrees F and line a baking sheet with parchment paper.

2. In a medium bowl, combine the flour, baking soda, and salt, and whisk well.

3. In the bowl of a stand mixer fitted with the paddle attachment, beat the butter with the sugars until light and fluffy, about 4 minutes, scraping down the sides of the bowl as needed. (You can also do this by hand, with a sturdy spoon.)

4. Add the eggs one at a time, beating between each addition. Add the peanut butter and vanilla, and beat on medium-low speed to blend. Add the dry ingredients in three batches, mixing on low speed until incorporated and scraping down the sides of the bowl as needed.

5. Using an ice cream scoop (mine has a capacity of about ¼ cup), scoop the dough onto the prepared baking sheet, taking care to leave about 2 inches between cookies.

6. Bake for 15 to 18 minutes, or until the cookies are puffed and pale golden around the edges. It is important that these cookies aren't fully baked, as the chewier they are, the better. And if you are freezing them for ice cream sandwiches, you won't want a crisp cookie—so be careful not to overbake!

7. Transfer the baking sheet to a rack, and cool the cookies completely on the sheet.

8. Repeat with the remaining dough.

note

This dough freezes great. Scoop the dough onto a baking sheet and freeze until hard; then transfer the cookies to a freezer bag or an airtight container. Do not defrost before baking; just add 4 or 5 minutes to the baking time.

salted peanut butter cookie ice cream sandwiches

Salted Peanut Butter Cookies (page 44) make fabulous ice cream sandwiches! To make, follow the cookie instructions. Once the cookies are perfectly cool, place a scoop of very cold vanilla (or chocolate) ice cream in the center of the bottom of a cookie. Place another cookie, top side up, over the ice cream and gently press down until the ice cream has spread nearly to the edge of both cookies. Repeat with the remaining cookies. Place in the freezer immediately, and freeze for at least 2 hours before enjoying. At this point, you can wrap the ice cream sandwiches in squares of parchment paper and seal with a cute personalized sticker.

fresh mint shake

INGREDIENTS

2 cups fresh mint leaves, packed

1 cup milk

½ cup honey

8 scoops Vanilla Ice Cream
(page 16) or store-bought

I love using fresh herbs in my dessert creations, so including this milk-shake in the book was a must. I decided to skip the classic chocolate-mint combo in favor of just mint and cream to really let the flavor of the fresh mint shine, but you could certainly use chocolate ice cream in place of the vanilla. I like to use blackberry honey, popular in the Northwest, although any honey will do.

Prep time: 1 hour 45 minutes | Active time: 10 minutes
Serves 4 in 6-ounce glasses

INSTRUCTIONS

1. Roughly chop the mint, including the stems, reserving a couple of leaves for garnish. The stems hold a lot of flavor, so be sure to include them.

2. In a small saucepan, warm the milk and honey over medium heat. When the milk has just reached a simmer, remove the pan from the heat and stir the mint into the milk, making sure all of it is submerged. Cover with a tightly fitting lid or plastic wrap and let the mint steep for 1 hour.

3. After the hour, using a fine mesh strainer (such as a chi-noise) over a bowl, squeeze all of the milk from the mint, either with your hands or using the back of a spoon. Discard the solids. The resulting liquid should be a beautiful pale green. Refrigerate the infused liquid until it is cool, about 30 minutes.

4. Blend the infused milk and ice cream until the ice cream is incorporated.

5. Pour into glasses and garnish with a mint leaf.

note
For extra minty-ness, add a drop of organic peppermint extract before blending. For extra yumminess, add about 6 chocolate cream sandwich cookies to the smooth milk-shake and blend lightly.

eggnog shake

Ah, the classic holiday drink most of us have come to love—a delicious combination of cream or milk, sugar, whipped eggs, and nutmeg. Interestingly enough, that is exactly the base of ice cream, sans the spices, so the Eggnog Shake's inclusion in this book was clear from the get-go. This milkshake is especially appreciated around the holidays, with a plate of sugar cookies perhaps, but it is good enough to be enjoyed throughout the year.

Note that this shake contains raw eggs. If you are uncomfortable consuming raw eggs, you may want to pass this one up.

Active time: 10 minutes

Serves 4 in 6-ounce glasses

INGREDIENTS

6 large egg yolks

½ cup heavy cream

¼ cup sugar

1¼ teaspoons freshly grated nutmeg, plus more for garnish

¾ teaspoon ground cloves

½ teaspoon ground cinnamon

8 scoops Vanilla Ice Cream (page 16) or store-bought

INSTRUCTIONS

1. Blend the egg yolks, cream, sugar, nutmeg, cloves, and cinnamon until thick and frothy. Add the ice cream and blend until just combined.

2. Pour into glasses and garnish with a sprinkling of freshly grated nutmeg. Enjoy!

note

For a boozy delight, add 2 tablespoons of good bourbon such as Woodford Reserve.

sweet cream and cookies shake

Cookies-and-cream is one of my favorite ice cream flavors and makes a delicious shake. This is my take on a classic. I really wanted to showcase the delicious flavor of fresh cream, and with the addition of milk powder and sour cream, the Sweet Cream and Cookies Shake gets the job done!

Active time: 10 minutes
Serves 4 in 6-ounce glasses

INGREDIENTS

½ cup milk

¼ cup heavy cream

¼ cup milk powder

2 teaspoons sugar

1 tablespoon sour cream, plus more for garnish

½ cup crumbled cookies (sandwich or chocolate chip work great), plus more for garnish

8 scoops Vanilla Ice Cream (page 16) or store-bought

INSTRUCTIONS

1. Blend the milk, heavy cream, milk powder, sugar, and sour cream until nice and smooth. Add the cookies and ice cream and blend until they are just combined.

2. Pour into glasses and garnish with a dollop of sour cream and a sprinkle of cookie crumbles.

tip
If you enjoy the extra-thick creaminess the heavy cream and sour cream lend to this shake, try swapping the cookies out for other fun, adventurous flavors—it's great with blueberry jam and fresh blueberries.

the blackstrap shake

INGREDIENTS

¾ cup milk

2 teaspoons finely grated fresh ginger

2 tablespoons finely chopped crystallized ginger, plus more for garnish

½ cup blackstrap or dark molasses

8 scoops Vanilla Ice Cream (page 16) or store-bought

½ cup crumbled gingersnap cookies

This milkshake combines healthy blackstrap molasses with ginger three ways. Little bits of crystallized ginger ignite when you bite into them, creating a rich, full, and spicy flavor that leaves your mouth pleasantly warm.

Molasses is a by-product of making sugar—it's what's left over after the boiling and crystallization process. Blackstrap molasses is from the sugar's third boil and contains trace amounts of nutrients, such as calcium, magnesium, potassium, and iron. If the flavor of blackstrap molasses is too intense, feel free to use a lighter molasses. For the cookies, I prefer a crisp Swedish-style gingersnap called MI-DEL, but you can use a chewy cookie if you prefer.

This shake is great at any time of year, but serving it next to a warm ginger cake might make the best holiday dessert ever.

Active time: 15 minutes
Serves 4 in 6-ounce glasses

INSTRUCTIONS

1. Blend the milk, fresh ginger, crystallized ginger, and molasses until they are nice and smooth. Add half of the ice cream and cookies and blend well.

2. Add the remaining ice cream and cookies and blend until they are just incorporated but still slightly chunky—this shake should have a varied texture.

3. Pour into glasses and garnish with a few pieces of crystallized ginger.

tip
Ginger Ice Cream (page 22) would be great in this shake instead of vanilla.

salted malted malt

The Salted Malted Malt is a classic malted vanilla with extra bells and whistles. The addition of heavy cream and salt and a hefty serving of malt powder make this shake a rich and powerful creamy delight!

Active time: 5 minutes
Serves 4 in 6-ounce glasses

INSTRUCTIONS

1. Blend the milk, cream, malt powder, salt, and vanilla until nice and smooth. Add the ice cream and blend until it is just incorporated.

2. Pour into glasses and enjoy!

INGREDIENTS

¼ cup milk

¼ cup heavy cream

½ cup plus 2 tablespoons malt powder

1 teaspoon kosher salt

½ teaspoon vanilla extract

8 scoops Vanilla Ice Cream (page 16) or store-bought

tip
You could also crumble cookies into this shake for a maltier, saltier version of cookies-and-cream.

passion fruit creamsicle shake

The first time I had passion fruit I was in Hawaii and ate it right from the tree, where it was perfectly ripe. I fell in love with its beautiful tart and floral flavor. You can usually find passion fruit in Asian markets or specialty food stores. Sometimes it can be a bit on the pricey side, but I think it is well worth it.

While not everybody chooses to eat the seeds, they add a lovely crunch to this shake. If you are using a blender, the seeds will break down, and you can use a straw to drink this shake. If you use a milkshake maker, like I did, the seeds will stay whole and then a spoon will be your best bet. Either way, you are in for a treat!

Active time: 10 minutes

Serves 4 in 6-ounce glasses

INSTRUCTIONS

1. Halve the passion fruits and scoop the pulp and seeds into a bowl. You should have about ½ cup of fruit pulp with seeds.

2. Blend the passion fruit pulp and seeds, sugar, cream, and ice cream until they are just combined.

3. Pour into glasses and garnish with whipped cream.

INGREDIENTS

4 passion fruits

¼ cup sugar

½ cup heavy cream

8 scoops Vanilla Ice Cream (page 16) or store-bought

1 recipe Lightly Whipped Cream (page 17), for garnish

modern flavors

EARL GREY SHAKE

SALTED CARAMEL SHAKE

PEANUT BUTTER AND
JELLY SHAKE

NOT YOUR GRANDMA'S
APPLE PIE SHAKE

SALT AND PEPPER MALT

S'MORES SHAKE

BACON–OATMEAL RAISIN
COOKIE SHAKE

MANGO ROSE SHAKE

BLACKBERRY LAVENDER SHAKE

STRAWBERRY CHEESECAKE SHAKE

WATERMELON LIME SHAKE

LEMON CURD
RASPBERRY SHAKE

MOLTEN CHOCOLATE
CAKE SHAKE

PEACH COBBLER SHAKE
OR MALT

SALTED BLACK LICORICE SHAKE

CHAI TEA SHAKE

TAMARIND SHAKE

TRUE CINNAMON SHAKE
OR MALT

earl grey shake

I love using Earl Grey tea in desserts. The essential oil of the bergamot orange adds a fragrant, citrus top note to the earthy, robust black tea. Because black tea has strong tannins, the steeping time for this shake is very important. Long extraction of the tea can lead to a bitter brew, so follow the steep time carefully.

This milkshake is sort of like a frozen London Fog—a drink made with Earl Grey, steamed milk, and vanilla syrup. I like to use honey in place of the vanilla syrup as it goes so nicely with the bergamot.

Prep time: 45 minutes | Active time: 10 minutes
Serves 4 in 6-ounce glasses

INGREDIENTS

1 ½ cups milk

½ cup honey

¼ cup plus 2 tablespoons loose Earl Grey tea leaves

2 tablespoons milk powder

8 scoops Vanilla Ice Cream (page 16) or store-bought

4 pieces orange zest, 2 inches long

note

This shake is delicious served with warm, gooey Molten Chocolate Cakes (page 90)!

INSTRUCTIONS

1. In a small saucepan, warm the milk and honey over medium heat. When the milk has just reached a simmer, remove the pan from the heat and add the tea leaves. Stir the tea into the milk, making sure all of it is submerged. Cover with a tightly fitting lid or plastic wrap and let the tea steep for 13 minutes.

2. Using a fine mesh strainer (such as a chinoise) over a bowl, squeeze all of the milk from the tea, either with your hands or using the back of a spoon. Discard the solids. Refrigerate the infused liquid until it is cool, about 30 minutes.

3. Blend the infused milk and milk powder until smooth. Add the ice cream and blend until just incorporated.

4. Pour into glasses. Roll each piece of orange zest tightly to release its oils, and drop one into each glass, fully submerging it. This will add a lovely hint of extra orange flavor.

salted caramel shake

Velvety smooth, delicious caramel spiked with a bit of sea salt creates a milkshake that will have you addicted. Salt and caramel make the perfect marriage: salt transforms the caramel by helping to neutralize its sweetness, rounding out the flavor and elevating the delicious smoky notes found only in a true caramel sauce.

Prep time: 45 minutes | Active time: 5 minutes
Serves 4 in 6-ounce glasses

INSTRUCTIONS

1. Blend the cooled caramel sauce, salt, and ice cream until the ice cream is just incorporated.

2. Pour into glasses and garnish with a drizzle of caramel sauce and a sprinkling of sea salt.

INGREDIENTS

1 cup Salted Caramel Sauce (recipe follows), plus more for garnish

¼ teaspoon salt

8 scoops Vanilla Ice Cream (page 16) or store-bought

Chunky sea salt, for garnish

note
Make extra Salted Caramel Sauce to keep in the fridge for sundaes, coffee, and fresh fruit.

INGREDIENTS

¾ cup heavy cream

¾ cup sugar

1 teaspoon salted butter, at room temperature

½ teaspoon salt

SALTED CARAMEL SAUCE

Most caramel sauce available on your grocery shelves isn't even real caramel, but rather what I like to call "faux caramel." The traditional technique for making caramel sauce is to caramelize, or begin to burn, the sugar. Because this method requires a skilled artisan and time, most manufacturers choose to make caramel sauce using a quicker, cheaper method. That method utilizes the Maillard reaction, in which the proteins in the milk or cream change flavor and color, mimicking those of caramelized sugar. But don't be fooled. The real deal is so much better.

Makes about 1 cup

INSTRUCTIONS

1. Warm the cream in a small saucepan over low heat. Meanwhile, in a heavy, medium sauté pan, melt the sugar over medium heat. As the sugar begins to liquefy, stir continually, as it will begin to change color and caramelize rather rapidly.

2. When the sugar has reached an even, light-amber color, watch for a bit of smoke to rise from it—this shows the sugar is caramelized. Immediately add the heated cream a little at a time, whisking after each addition.

3. Remove the pan from the heat and thoroughly whisk in the butter and salt, adding more salt if you prefer. Allow to cool completely.

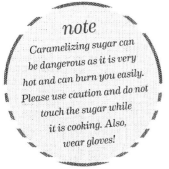

note
Caramelizing sugar can be dangerous as it is very hot and can burn you easily. Please use caution and do not touch the sugar while it is cooking. Also, wear gloves!

salted caramel sundae

If you are making caramel sauce, you might as well double the recipe and save some for Salted Caramel Sundaes, the deconstructed version of the milkshake with some extra goodness added for fun texture and flavor. If you have ingredients around the kitchen you think would be great toppers for this sundae, use them. That is the great thing about sundaes—they are so versatile.

Prep time: 45 minutes | Active time: 10 minutes
Makes 4 sundaes

8 scoops Vanilla Ice Cream (page 16) or store-bought

1 recipe Salted Caramel Sauce (page 60), warm

1 recipe Rye Crumble (page 103)

1 recipe Lightly Whipped Cream (page 17)

1 cup Brandied Cherries (page 116) or good-quality natural maraschino cherries

Chunky sea salt, for garnish

1. Place 4 sundae dishes in the freezer 20 minutes prior to assembling the sundaes.

2. Place two scoops of ice cream in each frosted dish. Top generously with caramel sauce, crumble, whipped cream, and finally, cherries. Garnish with a light sprinkling of sea salt.

tip
You can kick the deliciousness up a notch if you use salted caramel ice cream instead of vanilla. If you can't find it at your local store, not to worry—vanilla does the job beautifully.

peanut butter and jelly shake

Don't think for a second this shake is just for kids. Of course, your kids will love it, but it will knock the socks off guests of all ages at a summertime barbecue. The Peanut Butter and Jelly Shake works with any kind of berry syrup: just replace the strawberries with your preferred berry. You can also use jam if you are crunched for time.

Prep time: 30 minutes | Active time: 5 minutes
Serves 4 in 6-ounce glasses

INSTRUCTIONS

1. To make the peanut butter swirl: Warm the water and sugar in a small saucepan over medium heat. While stirring, bring the mixture to a boil, then remove the pan from the heat. This is simple syrup. Measure out ¼ cup of the syrup and whisk it into the oil and peanut butter in a small bowl. Allow to cool.

2. To make the toasted bread crumbles: Preheat the oven (a toaster oven works great for this) to 400 degrees F. Butter one side of each bread slice, sprinkle with a bit of salt, and place the bread on your oven rack. Bake until the slices are dark golden brown, and the edges are slightly darker. The bread should be crisp throughout, no soft spots. Let the slices cool, then use a knife or your fingers to crumble them into roughly pea-size pieces.

3. To make the shake: Blend the milk and ice cream until it is just incorporated. Fill each glass halfway with the shake mixture. Then scoop some strawberry syrup and peanut butter swirl into each glass. Pour the remaining shake mixture over the peanut butter swirl and strawberry syrup.

4. Garnish with a drizzle of both the strawberry syrup and the peanut butter swirl, and a generous portion of toasted bread crumbles. This shake is best eaten with a spoon!

INGREDIENTS

PEANUT BUTTER SWIRL

¼ cup water

¼ cup sugar

3 tablespoons peanut oil

½ cup creamy, salted, natural peanut butter

TOASTED BREAD CRUMBLES

2 slices day-old French or other bread

Butter for buttering the bread

Kosher salt

SHAKE

½ cup milk

8 scoops Vanilla Ice Cream (page 16) or store-bought

2 cups Strawberry Syrup (page 34)

INGREDIENTS

APPLES

1 small Granny Smith apple, peeled, cored, and diced into ¼-inch cubes

1 tablespoon unsalted butter

1 tablespoon brown sugar

SHAKE

¾ cup apple cider or juice

¼ teaspoon ground cinnamon, plus more for garnish

¼ teaspoon ground cardamom

⅛ teaspoon ground cloves

⅛ teaspoon ground nutmeg

¼ teaspoon vanilla extract

2 teaspoons finely grated fresh ginger

8 scoops Vanilla Ice Cream (page 16) or store-bought

1 recipe Lightly Whipped Cream, (page 17)

not your grandma's apple pie shake

We make the best apple pie ever at Hot Cakes! By using fresh ginger and cardamom, Not Your Grandma's Apple Pie Shake makes the average apple pie into something special. This shake is fun to have with a slice of warm apple pie—no need for à la mode!

Prep time: 30 minutes | Active time: 5 minutes
Serves 4 in 6-ounce glasses

INSTRUCTIONS

1. To make the apples: In a small sauté pan over medium heat, cook the apples, butter, and brown sugar until the apples are soft but still have a bite to them, about 4 minutes. Allow the apples and syrup to cool completely.

2. To make the shake: In a blender, blend the cider, cinnamon, cardamom, cloves, nutmeg, vanilla, and ginger until they are nice and smooth.

3. Add the ice cream and blend until it is just incorporated. Stir in the cooked apples, reserving a few cubes for garnish, along with the buttery syrup from the pan.

4. Pour into glasses and garnish with a dollop of whipped cream, some apple cubes, and a dusting of cinnamon.

apple pocket pies

Apple pie is America's favorite dessert. It is fun to spruce it up a bit with different spices and fruit, and put the filling in a cute little pocket, perfect for a handheld treat. At Hot Cakes, we call our hand-pies Pocket Pies. They do fit right in your pocket—but be careful, they smush easily!

Prep time: 1 hour | Active time: 1 ½ hours

PIE DOUGH

3 cups all-purpose flour

1 teaspoon salt

1 teaspoon sugar

2½ sticks very cold unsalted butter, cut into ½-inch cubes

¼ cup ice water

APPLE FILLING

4 pounds Granny Smith apples, peeled, cored, and cut into ⅛-inch-thick slices

2 cups plus 2 tablespoons sugar

1½ cups brown sugar, packed

⅓ cup cornstarch

1¼ teaspoons ground cardamom

1¼ teaspoons ground cinnamon

1 tablespoon finely grated fresh ginger

½ teaspoon ground nutmeg

1¼ teaspoons freshly squeezed lemon juice

1 teaspoon vanilla extract

½ teaspoon salt

EGG WASH

1 large egg

Makes 8 to 10 pocket pies

1. To make the pie dough: Combine the flour, salt, and sugar in the bowl of a stand mixer. Using a whisk or fork, stir until evenly combined.

2. Break up the butter with your fingers and add it to the flour mixture. Using the paddle attachment, mix on low-medium until the mixture begins to resemble peas. (You can also do this by hand, with a sturdy fork or pastry cutter.) Stop the mixer and, with your

fingers, break up any large pieces of butter. Resume mixing until the dough just barely begins to stick together, then quickly add the water in a steady stream. Mix again until the dough is just beginning to stick to the paddle. (Note that you will be mixing the dough just a bit longer than you normally would for a dish pie, as you will need to form a little more gluten to create a dough strong enough to withstand the pocket form.)

3. Form the dough into a ball, making sure to knead out any air pockets. Your dough ball should be uniform without any cracks or holes. Flatten it into a 1-inch-thick disc, then cover it well with plastic wrap and refrigerate for at least 3 hours and up to 1 day.

4. While the dough chills, prepare the apple filling.

5. To make the apple filling: Preheat the oven to 350 degrees F. In a large metal bowl, combine the apples, sugar, brown sugar, cornstarch, cardamom, cinnamon, nutmeg, ginger, lemon juice, vanilla, and salt. Using your hands, mix until everything is well combined. Pour the apple mixture into an 11-by-8-inch glass baking dish or similar, and cover with aluminum foil. Bake until the juices are bubbly and the apples are soft, about 1 hour.

6. Allow the filling to cool completely before making the pies.

7. Remove the dough from the refrigerator and let it sit on the counter for 30 minutes.

8. To assemble the pocket pies, lightly flour a work surface. With a rolling pin, roll the dough out into a big rectangle about $\frac{1}{8}$ inch thick. Using a ruler and knife, cut the dough into rectangles that measure approximately $4\frac{1}{2}$ by 8 inches. (You can reroll the scraps for extra rectangles, but the dough's texture will be a bit more tough and chewy.)

9. To make the egg wash: In a small bowl, beat the egg really well until it is foamy and smooth.

10. Line up three dough rectangles in front of you. Using a pastry brush, brush a thin strip (about $\frac{1}{2}$ inch wide) of egg wash onto the

edges of the rectangles' long sides. Be sure to avoid getting egg into the middle of the dough, or the pocket will stick together and you won't be able to get any filling in there.

11. Fold the upper half of the rectangle over the bottom half, creating a square. Using the tips of your fingers, firmly press two out of three open edges together, creating a tight seal. One of the edges should be left open, making a pocket. Using a fork, crimp the sealed edges, going in about $\frac{3}{4}$ inch. Repeat with the remaining dough rectangles. Be sure to form all of the pockets before you begin to fill them—it takes about 5 minutes for the seal to properly adhere, and waiting will ensure the pies don't leak.

12. To fill the pockets, pick one up in the palm of your hand. Be careful not to hold it for too long, as you don't want the butter in the dough to melt. Spoon some filling into the pocket, packing it down gently into the corners and being careful not to get it on the top inside edges, where you will need to create a seal. Leave about 1 inch of room at the top of the pocket; don't fill it totally. Brush egg wash along the top inside edge. Firmly press the two pieces together, squeezing out any air as you go along. Pinch the edges shut and crimp with a fork as you did above. Once you have finished all of the pockets, cut a slit in the top and brush egg wash over the top and edges. Refrigerate the pies for at least 1 hour before baking.

13. Note: At this point, you can freeze the pies on a baking sheet, making sure they are not touching each other. Once they are frozen, transfer them to an airtight container where they will keep for up to 6 months. Bake as directed below. Do not defrost before baking; just add about 7 minutes to the baking time.

14. To bake your pies, preheat the oven to 350 degrees F. Arrange the pies 2 inches apart on a baking sheet lined with parchment paper. Bake for 30–35 minutes or until the pies are golden brown and some of the filling is bubbling from the slit.

15. Cool the pies for at least 20 minutes before devouring!

salt and pepper malt

Black pepper not only gives this shake a kick but also lends lovely floral notes. Be sure to use either whole peppercorns or freshly ground black pepper—preground pepper loses its flavor and floral notes rapidly.

Active time: 10 minutes
Serves 4 in 6-ounce glasses

INSTRUCTIONS

1. Blend the milk, pepper, salt, and malt powder until nice and smooth. If you are using whole peppercorns, make sure they are well blended.

2. Add the ice creams and blend until they are just incorporated.

3. Pour into glasses and garnish with a little pepper and a sprinkle of salt.

INGREDIENTS

$^3/_4$ cup milk

2 teaspoons whole black peppercorns, or $^3/_4$ teaspoon freshly ground black pepper, plus more ground pepper for garnish

1 teaspoon kosher salt, plus more for garnish

$^1/_2$ cup malt powder

4 scoops Vanilla Ice Cream (page 16) or store-bought

4 scoops Chocolate Ice Cream (page 18) or store-bought

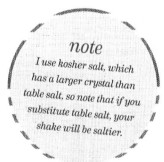

note
I use kosher salt, which has a larger crystal than table salt, so note that if you substitute table salt, your shake will be saltier.

s'mores shake

I was a Girl Scout for many years. In troop 1492 we were always so busy having fun I'm not sure if we ever got around to making s'mores, but the classic treat is said to be invented by the Girl Scouts. The S'mores Shake calls for roasted marshmallows, which requires some kind of a flame. If you don't have a gas stove or torch, you can use the broiler in your oven. Just be sure to watch the marshmallows closely and use greased aluminum foil on your baking sheet.

Prep time: 45 minutes | Active time: 5 minutes
Serves 4 in 6-ounce glasses

INGREDIENTS

2 tablespoons unsalted butter

8 marshmallows, roasted until very dark

¼ cup milk

8 scoops Vanilla Ice Cream (page 16) or store-bought

½ cup crumbled graham crackers, plus more for garnish

2 tablespoons melted Chocolate Ice Cream (page 18) or store-bought

INSTRUCTIONS

1. In a medium saucepan over medium heat, melt the butter. Add the marshmallows and stir until they melt and the mixture is smooth.

2. Remove the pan from the heat and pour in the milk, stirring until the mixture is again smooth. Cool completely. (Note: If the marshmallow milk sits for too long, it will become very stiff. Prepare it within an hour of when you are going to make the shakes.)

3. Blend the marshmallow milk with the vanilla ice cream until they are just combined.

4. Stir in the crumbled graham crackers and gently swirl the melted chocolate ice cream throughout.

5. Pour into glasses and garnish with a sprinkle of graham crackers.

INGREDIENTS

1 cup milk

½ cup raisins

¾ cup Bacon–Oatmeal Raisin Cookie chunks (recipe follows)

8 scoops Vanilla Ice Cream (page 16) or store-bought

bacon–oatmeal raisin cookie shake

It may sound crazy to put bacon in your oatmeal raisin cookies, but you'll soon see why we do it at Hot Cakes. Bacon paired with its breakfast counterparts oatmeal and raisins creates the perfect cookie, with hints of savory smokiness. We adapted our recipe just for this milkshake.

Prep time: 1 hour | Active time: 5 minutes
Serves 4 in 6-ounce glasses

INSTRUCTIONS

1. In a small saucepan, bring the milk to a simmer over medium heat. Remove the pan from the heat and add the raisins.

2. Cover the pan with a tight-fitting lid or plastic wrap and let the milk sit for 1 hour.

3. Blend the milk and raisins until they are mostly smooth. Add the cookie chunks and ice cream and blend until they are just incorporated, but still chunky. (You may need to scrape down the sides of the blender.)

4. Pour into glasses and enjoy!

INGREDIENTS

One 12-ounce package bacon

3 cups all-purpose or pastry flour

$\frac{3}{4}$ teaspoon baking soda

$\frac{1}{2}$ teaspoon baking powder

$1\frac{1}{2}$ teaspoons salt

$1\frac{1}{2}$ sticks unsalted butter

$1\frac{1}{2}$ cups dark brown sugar, packed

$\frac{1}{2}$ cup sugar

2 large eggs

$\frac{3}{4}$ teaspoon vanilla extract

$1\frac{1}{4}$ cups old-fashioned rolled oats

$1\frac{1}{4}$ cups raisins

BACON–OATMEAL RAISIN COOKIES

My dad used to put bacon in our waffles. And we used to top our oatmeal with it too. So it was only natural for me to turn a standard oatmeal raisin cookie into a nostalgic and delicious homage to my childhood.

Makes about 20 four-inch cookies

INSTRUCTIONS

1. Preheat the oven to 350 degrees F and line a baking sheet with parchment paper.

2. In a frying pan over medium heat, cook the bacon until crispy. Transfer the bacon to a paper-towel-lined plate and reserve $\frac{1}{4}$ cup of the bacon fat, discarding the rest. Allow the bacon and the bacon fat to cool, then chop the bacon into roughly $\frac{1}{2}$-inch pieces.

3. In a medium bowl, combine the flour, baking soda, baking powder, and salt, and whisk well.

4. In the bowl of a stand mixer fitted with the paddle attachment, beat the butter and reserved bacon fat with the brown sugar and sugar until light and fluffy, about 4 minutes, scraping down the sides of the bowl as needed. (You can also do this by hand, with a sturdy spoon.)

5. Add the eggs one at a time, beating between each addition. Add the vanilla, and beat on medium-low speed to blend.

6. Add the dry ingredients in three batches, mixing on low speed until incorporated and scraping down the sides of the bowl as needed.

7. Stir in the bacon, oats, and raisins until evenly incorporated.

8. Using an ice cream scoop (mine has a capacity of about ¼ cup), scoop the dough onto the prepared baking sheet, taking care to leave about 2 inches of space between cookies. Bake for approximately 17 minutes, or until the cookies are puffed and golden around the edges. The centers of the cookies will be slightly gooey when they come out of the oven. If you like your cookies a bit crisper, feel free to leave them in the oven for another few minutes.

9. Cool them on the baking sheet for at least 5 minutes before transferring them to the counter or a rack to cool completely. Repeat with the remaining dough.

note

This dough freezes great. Scoop the dough onto a baking sheet and freeze until hard; then transfer the cookies to a freezer bag or an airtight container. Do not defrost before baking; just add 4 or 5 minutes to the baking time.

bacon–oatmeal raisin cookie ice cream sandwiches

Bacon–Oatmeal Raisin Cookies (page 74) make fantastic ice cream sandwiches! To make, follow the cookie instructions. Once the cookies are perfectly cool, place a scoop of very cold vanilla (or salted caramel—my favorite) ice cream in the center of the bottom of a cookie. Place another cookie, top side up, over the ice cream and gently press down until the ice cream has spread nearly to the edge of both cookies. Repeat with the remaining cookies. Place in the freezer immediately, and freeze for at least 2 hours before enjoying. At this point, you can wrap the ice cream sandwiches in squares of parchment paper and seal with a cute personalized sticker.

mango rose shake

The mango plays a supporting role to the bright bouquet of the rose water in this shake. It boasts a beautiful pale orange color and has an equally subtle yet profound flavor.

Rose hydrosol, or rose water, is what is left over when making rose essential oil. You can find a pure, food-grade source at apothecaries and some specialty food stores.

Active time: 15 minutes
Serves 4 in 6-ounce glasses

INSTRUCTIONS

1. Blend the mango, cream, milk, sugar, rose water, and salt until smooth. Add ice cream and blend until just combined.

2. Pour into glasses and enjoy!

INGREDIENTS

1 large fresh mango, peeled, pitted, and cut into $\frac{1}{2}$-inch pieces (about $\frac{3}{4}$ cup)

$\frac{1}{3}$ cup heavy cream

$\frac{1}{3}$ cup milk

3 tablespoons sugar

1 tablespoon rose water or rose hydrosol

$\frac{1}{4}$ teaspoon salt

8 scoops Vanilla Ice Cream (page 16) or store-bought

note
This recipe is similar to a mango lassi. If you like the tang of a lassi, try adding plain yogurt instead of the heavy cream.

blackberry lavender shake

The first wedding cake I ever made was lavender chiffon with blackberry pie filling and cream cheese icing. My friend and I gathered the lavender and spent a whole day picking blackberries from my uncle's yard. Since then, the combination of blackberries and lavender, both proud Northwest ingredients, has become a staple in my dessert kitchen. The candied lavender in this shake bursts like little gems of delightful flavor.

Prep time: 30 minutes | Active time: 5 minutes
Serves 4 in 6-ounce glasses

INGREDIENTS

¾ cup milk

1 tablespoon sugar

3 tablespoons dried lavender flowers

8 scoops Vanilla Ice Cream (page 16) or store-bought

1 recipe Candied Lavender (recipe follows)

1 cup chopped fresh or frozen blackberries, thawed

INSTRUCTIONS

1. In a small saucepan, warm the milk and sugar over medium heat. When the milk has just reached a simmer, remove the pan from the heat and add the lavender flowers, stirring them into the milk making sure they are all submerged.

2. Cover the pan with a tightly fitting lid or plastic wrap, and let the lavender steep for 15 minutes.

3. Using a fine mesh strainer (such as a chinoise) over a bowl, squeeze all of the milk from the lavender, either with your hands or using the back of a spoon. It should be a beautiful pale purple/gray color. Allow the milk to cool.

4. Blend the infused milk and ice cream until the ice cream is just incorporated. Stir in the candied lavender, reserving some for garnish, and the blackberries.

5. Pour into glasses and garnish with a sprinkle of candied lavender.

note
You can purchase dried lavender flowers in most spice shops. You can also order online or just pick from your garden!

INGREDIENTS

4 tablespoons sugar, divided

1 tablespoon water

2 tablespoons dried lavender flowers

CANDIED LAVENDER

Leftover candied lavender can be stored in an airtight container for a few weeks; try using it in shortbread cookies or as a salad garnish. It is also delicious on its own!

Makes ¼ cup

INSTRUCTIONS

1. Spread 2 tablespoons of the sugar on a cutting board.

2. Pour the water into a small sauté pan, add the remaining 2 tablespoons sugar, and cook over medium heat; most of the sugar will dissolve, and the syrup should bubble. Cook, stirring, for 1 minute, then add the lavender flowers.

3. Continue to cook as the syrup bubbles, stirring occasionally, for 2 minutes; there should be very little liquid left in the pan at this point. No need to worry about the syrup crystallizing—this is what you want.

4. Immediately pour the lavender syrup mixture onto the sugar on the cutting board. Using a spoon, coat the lavender with sugar; once it is cool enough to touch, use your fingers to break up the chunks. The sugar should coat each individual flower, but it is OK to have little flower clusters.

strawberry cheesecake shake

Growing up, I always ordered strawberry cheesecake when eating out. What's not to love? Super creamy and slightly tangy with homemade strawberry syrup, this shake plays up the delicious flavors of the classic treat.

Prep time: 30 minutes | Active time: 5 minutes
Serves 4 in 6-ounce glasses

INSTRUCTIONS

1. Blend the milk, cream cheese, and vanilla until smooth and frothy. Add the ice cream and blend until it is just incorporated.

2. Gently swirl in the strawberry syrup.

3. Pour into glasses and garnish with the graham crackers. You may want to use a spoon for this one!

INGREDIENTS

¼ cup milk

¼ cup cream cheese, softened

¼ teaspoon vanilla extract

8 scoops Vanilla Ice Cream (page 16) or store-bought

1 cup Strawberry Syrup (page 34)

Crumbled graham crackers, for garnish

tip
Take care to blend the milk and cream cheese thoroughly.

watermelon lime shake

INGREDIENTS

One 3-to 5-pound watermelon

¼ cup plus 2 tablespoons sugar

½ teaspoon salt

¼ cup plus 1 tablespoon freshly squeezed lime juice (from about 3 medium limes)

12 scoops Vanilla Ice Cream (page 16) or store-bought

4 paper-thin lime slices

The watermelon flavor is subtle, and the lime is a zingy, refreshing complement, making this the best picnic milkshake ever. Try to find the ripest, juiciest, and sweetest watermelon around. If you are using a watermelon with seeds, try to pick out most of them, but leaving a few is OK; they will get chopped up and lend a pretty, black speckle to the shake.

Active time: 15 minutes
Serves 4 in 8-ounce glasses

INSTRUCTIONS

1. Remove the rind from the watermelon and cut the fruit into enough 1-inch pieces to measure 4 cups and enough ¼-inch pieces to measure 2 cups.

2. Blend the 4 cups of watermelon with the sugar, salt, and lime juice until the watermelon is completely liquid. Add the ice cream and blend until it is just combined.

3. Stir in the 2 cups of smaller watermelon pieces.

4. Pour into glasses and garnish with a lime wedge.

note
Because this shake is so light, I serve it in an 8-ounce glass.

lemon curd raspberry shake

Lemon Curd Raspberry Shake is in my top three for sure. The egg yolks in the curd create a texture that can only be compared to the softest velvet. This shake is such a gorgeous pale yellow too—perfect for a summer after-noon or an outdoor dinner party. I found that while I love this shake with the raspberries, it is delicious without them too.

Prep time: 30 minutes | Active time: 5 minutes
Serves 4 in 6-ounce glasses

INSTRUCTIONS

1. In a small bowl, combine the raspberries and sugar. Macer-ate the berries by tossing them in the sugar and allowing them to sit while you make the lemon curd.

2. Blend the lemon curd, milk, and ice cream until they are mostly combined. Stir in the macerated raspberries.

3. Pour into glasses and garnish with a dollop of whipped cream and a lemon slice.

INGREDIENTS

$\frac{1}{2}$ cup fresh or frozen raspberries, thawed

$\frac{1}{4}$ cup sugar

1 recipe Lemon Curd (recipe follows)

$\frac{1}{4}$ cup milk

8 scoops Vanilla Ice Cream (page 16) or store-bought

1 recipe Lightly Whipped Cream (page 17)

4 paper-thin lemon slices

note
If you don't have raspberries on hand, don't let it stop you from making this luxuriously creamy lemony delight.

INGREDIENTS

4 large egg yolks

$\frac{1}{2}$ cup plus 2 tablespoons sugar

$\frac{1}{2}$ cup plus 2 tablespoons freshly squeezed lemon juice (from about 2 large lemons)

$\frac{1}{2}$ stick unsalted butter, cut into $\frac{1}{2}$-inch pieces

LEMON CURD

Lemon curd is a classic spread traditionally used on toast and scones. But really the possibilities are endless for this zesty treat. If you have leftovers, they will keep in the fridge, covered for a few weeks.

Makes about 1 cup

INSTRUCTIONS

1. In a small metal bowl, whisk the egg yolks and sugar until fluffy and pale. Whisk in the lemon juice. Fill a small saucepan with $\frac{1}{2}$ inch of water. Warm the water over medium-high heat until it is simmering.

2. Set the metal bowl with the yolk mixture over the simmering water (the bowl should not touch the water). Stirring continually with a wooden spoon, cook the yolk mixture for approximately 4 minutes, or until it coats the back of the spoon. Be careful not to overcook: you don't want sweet, lemony scrambled eggs.

3. Quickly remove the bowl from the saucepan and begin adding the butter in pieces, stirring after each addition, until the butter is melted and well incorporated. Cool before using.

lemon-ginger-maple sundaes

This dessert's inspiration comes from the popular tonic of lemon juice, fresh ginger, maple syrup, and cayenne. It's great to drink if you think you may be coming down with something, but this sundae is good no matter how you are feeling! The addition of the cayenne gives this treat a great kick, but feel free to leave it out.

Active time: 10 minutes

Makes 4 sundaes

8 scoops Ginger Ice Cream (page 22) or store-bought

8 tablespoons real maple syrup

1 cup Lemon Curd (page 86)

2 recipes Lightly Whipped Cream (page 17)

½ cup crushed gingersnap cookies

Chunky sea salt, for garnish

Cayenne, for garnish

1. Place 4 sundae dishes in the freezer at least 20 minutes prior to assembling the sundaes.

2. Place two scoops of ice cream in each frosted dish, and drizzle with 2 tablespoons of maple syrup. Divide the lemon curd among the dishes, spooning it over the top of the ice cream.

3. Top the curd with a dollop of whipped cream and a heavy sprinkling of crushed ginger snaps.

4. Garnish each sundae with a pinch of salt and cayenne. Enjoy!

molten chocolate cake shake

Hot Cakes Confections was founded on the tried-and-true classic dessert. Its rich, gooey, chocolaty center makes people happy every time. Since molten chocolate cake is served warm and milkshakes are cold, the Molten Chocolate Cake Shake requires a few stages: first, make the molten chocolate cakes and cool them, then break them up into pieces and stir them throughout the shake. Next, make the ganache and pour that into the middle of the shake for the effect of a gooey center! This shake is so thick with chocolaty goodness, you will need a spoon to enjoy it. For a really decadent option, you can always serve the cakes alongside the shake.

Prep time: 2 hours | Active time: 20 minutes
Serves 4 in 6-ounce glasses

INSTRUCTIONS

1. To make the ganache: Warm the cream in a small saucepan over medium heat. When it begins to simmer around the edges, remove the pan from the heat and add the chocolate chips.

2. Let the ganache sit for 1 minute, then stir until the chips are fully melted. Cool on the counter or in the refrigerator.

3. To make the shake: Blend the molten cake, milk, and ice cream until just incorporated.

4. Pour into glasses. Garnish with a little drizzle of ganache into the center of each glass.

INGREDIENTS

GANACHE

½ cup heavy cream

¼ cup plus 1 tablespoon dark chocolate chips

SHAKE

1 Molten Chocolate Cake (recipe follows), cooled and broken into small pieces

½ cup milk

8 scoops Chocolate Ice Cream (page 18) or store-bought

INGREDIENTS

Butter for greasing ramekins

1¼ cups dark chocolate chips or dark chocolate, chopped into small pieces

¼ teaspoon salt

3 large egg whites

⅓ cup sugar, divided in two

5 large egg yolks

¼ cup cocoa powder

MOLTEN CHOCOLATE CAKES

Molten cakes are classic. If you like chocolate, what's not to love about a warm cake with a gooey center? They are the dessert that Hot Cakes was founded on, and the flavor possibilities are endless!

Makes 4 cakes

INSTRUCTIONS

1. Preheat the oven to 350 degrees F.

2. Prepare four 4-ounce ramekins by buttering the bottom and inside walls well. Refrigerate until needed.

3. Melt the chocolate in the microwave, or fill a small saucepan with ½ inch of water. Warm the water over medium-high heat until it is simmering. Set a small metal bowl with the chocolate over the simmering water (the bowl should not touch the water), stirring constantly until the chocolate is melted. Set aside.

4. In the bowl of a stand mixer, combine the salt, egg whites, and half of the sugar, set aside. In a medium metal bowl, combine the remaining sugar, egg yolks, and cocoa powder and whisk well. Again, set the bowl over a small saucepan filled with ½ inch of simmering water. Whisk until the yolks are very warm to the touch, and the sugar has melted; set aside.

5. Using the whisk attachment, immediately beat the egg white mixture until it forms medium-stiff peaks.

6. At this point, the temperature of the yolks and the chocolate should still be warm. If either has cooled off, you will need to reheat it before the next step.

7. Fold the yolks into the whites until evenly incorporated. Fit the mixing bowl with the paddle attachment and, on low speed, slowly add the chocolate in a steady stream close to the edge of the bowl. Be sure to periodically scrape down the paddle and mixing bowl, as the chocolate has a tendency to adhere, and every little bit matters in this recipe! Increase the speed to medium-low and mix until the batter is smooth.

8. Pour the batter evenly among the prepared ramekins and place them on the middle rack of the oven. (At this point, the batter can be frozen; see note below.) Bake the cakes for about 12 minutes: the tops should puff into a slight dome, and a crack or two will appear. The center should be gooey so don't overbake! If you are at high elevation or baking frozen batter, you will need to increase the baking time by a few minutes.

9. Remove the cakes from the oven with tongs and, if using them for the milkshake, cool them completely on the counter. If eating them immediately, invert them onto serving plates, allow them to cool for a minute before removing the ramekin, and garnish as desired.

note

You can refrigerate the batter in the ramekins, tightly covered, to use at a later time. It will keep for up to 2 weeks in the refrigerator or 6 months in the freezer.

molten cake à la mode

If you are excited about making Molten Chocolate Cakes, but not so excited about using them in a milkshake, a quick and delicious way to spruce up your warm, gooey cake is with a good dousing of salted caramel sauce, unsweetened whipped cream, and a sprinkle of sea salt, as we do at Hot Cakes.

Prep time: 1 hour | Active time: 20 minutes

Makes 4 desserts

1 recipe Salted Caramel Sauce (page 60)

1 recipe Molten Chocolate Cakes (page 90)

1 recipe unsweetened Lightly Whipped Cream (page 17)

Sea salt, for garnish

1. Pour about $\frac{1}{4}$ cup caramel sauce over each cake and top with whipped cream and a sprinkle of sea salt. Eat right away!

peach cobbler shake or malt

There is nothing like a warm, buttery and bubbly peach cobbler made with juicy ripe peaches. Peaches are one of those fruits that are almost always better when eaten fresh and raw, but magic happens when the peach is baked cobbler-style. This shake captures the best of both worlds—it is kind of a deconstructed, blended cobbler with fresh peaches and a baked crumble top. The trick is to find the ripest, juiciest, most flavorful peaches around!

Prep time: 20 minutes | Active time: 10 minutes
Serves 4 in 6-ounce glasses

INSTRUCTIONS

1. To make the crumble: Melt the butter in a medium sauté pan over medium-low heat, then stir in the brown sugar until they are evenly combined.

2. Add the flour, oats, and salt, and cook, stirring frequently and making sure not to burn the flour. The crumble is done when it starts to smell toasty, about 3 to 5 minutes. Transfer it immediately to a plate to cool.

3. To make the shake: Blend the milk, sugar, sour cream, and vanilla extract until smooth. Add the peaches and ice cream and blend until just incorporated.

4. Pour into glasses and garnish with a heavy layer of crumble. This shake is best eaten with a straw/spoon combo.

INGREDIENTS

CRUMBLE

2 tablespoons unsalted butter

¼ cup brown sugar, packed

¼ cup all-purpose flour

¼ cup old-fashioned rolled oats

¼ teaspoon salt

SHAKE

½ cup milk

¼ cup plus 2 tablespoons sugar

2 tablespoons sour cream

1 teaspoon vanilla extract

1 large ripe peach, cut into ½-inch slices (about 1 cup)

8 scoops Vanilla Ice Cream (page 16) or store-bought

note
This recipe is delicious as a malt! Just add 2 tablespoons of malt powder to the milk and blend well.

salted black licorice shake

My mom loves the really hard-to-find, extra-salty black licorice. While it makes my lips pucker and my mouth go numb, I do appreciate it, and I certainly appreciate black licorice. This shake is a happy medium between extra salty and mildly salty. Feel free to adjust the salt levels to your heart's content.

Prep time: 1 hour | Active time: 5 minutes
Serves 4 in 6-ounce glasses

INGREDIENTS

1 cup milk

½ cup natural soft black licorice candy, cut into ¼-inch pieces

1 teaspoon kosher salt

8 scoops Vanilla Ice Cream (page 16) or store-bought

INSTRUCTIONS

1. In a small saucepan, warm the milk over medium heat. When it has just reached a simmer, remove the pan from the heat and add the licorice, stirring it into the milk and making sure all of it is submerged.

2. Cover the pan with a tightly fitting lid or plastic wrap and let the licorice steep for 1 hour.

3. Blend the licorice and milk for a couple of minutes. There will still be some small pieces that won't break up, but this is OK, as the chunks give the shake so much character!

4. Add the salt, adding more if you prefer, and ice cream and blend until they are just combined.

5. Pour into glasses and enjoy!

note

I use natural black licorice, which is colored with natural ingredients. Conventional black licorice is dyed with food coloring, which will cause your shake to turn green. So, if possible, purchase the natural black licorice.

chai tea shake

INGREDIENTS

1 cup milk

2 tablespoons green cardamom pods

2 teaspoons black peppercorns

½ teaspoon ground nutmeg

¼ teaspoon ground cloves

1 teaspoon ground cinnamon, plus more for garnish

1½ teaspoons chopped fresh ginger

2 tablespoons black tea

3 tablespoons sugar

8 scoops Vanilla Ice Cream (page 16) or store-bought

1 recipe Lightly Whipped Cream (page 17), for garnish

In most of the world, the word "chai" refers to tea. But here in the States, when we say chai, we are referring to the eastern Indian tea beverage that is delightfully laced with spices, sugar, and milk. I prefer my chai with a bit of a kick, so I like a lot of ginger and black peppercorns. Note that we are making a chai concentrate below so it will taste bitter on its own, but when blended with the ice cream, it mellows beautifully.

Prep time: 30 minutes | Active time: 10 minutes
Serves 4 in 6-ounce glasses

INSTRUCTIONS

1. In a small saucepan, warm the milk over medium heat. When it has just reached a simmer, add the cardamom, peppercorns, nutmeg, cloves, cinnamon, and ginger, stirring the spices into the milk and making sure all are submerged.

2. Reduce the heat to low and let the milk simmer for 5 minutes. Add the black tea and simmer for another 5 minutes.

3. Remove the pan from the heat and, using a fine mesh strainer (such as a chinoise) over a bowl, squeeze all of the milk from the tea and spices, either with your hands or using the back of a spoon. Discard the solids. Add the sugar to the milk and stir until it is completely dissolved. Allow to cool.

4. Blend the milk with the ice cream until they are just combined.

5. Pour into glasses and garnish with a dollop of lightly whipped cream and a dash of cinnamon.

tamarind shake

Tamarind is a seriously tart fruit that originally hails from Africa. It is grown all over the world now and used in many culinary applications. I first discovered it as the main ingredient in pad thai sauce but then had the pleasure of tasting it ripe from the tree in Spain. Tamarind paste can be found in most grocery stores and Asian markets. It really packs a sour punch, so it is best paired with sugar or lots of salt. It also pairs nicely with orange, so I have included a dab of sweet orange oil in this shake.

Active time: 5 minutes

Serves 4 in 6-ounce glasses

INSTRUCTIONS

1. Blend the milk, tamarind, sugar, and orange oil until smooth. Add the ice cream and blend until just incorporated.

2. Pour into glasses and enjoy!

INGREDIENTS

$\frac{1}{2}$ cup milk

2 tablespoons tamarind concentrate or paste

$\frac{1}{4}$ cup sugar

2 drops sweet orange essential oil

8 scoops Vanilla Ice Cream (page 16) or store-bought

note

Orange essential oil is far superior to orange extract, so seek it out—it's worth it. You can find it in any apothecary, health food store, or online.

true cinnamon shake or malt

INGREDIENTS

½ cup milk

2 tablespoons sugar

1 tablespoon ground true cinnamon, plus more for garnish

8 scoops Vanilla Ice Cream (page 16) or store-bought

True cinnamon, or Ceylon cinnamon, is not your common cinnamon. The cinnamon most of us use in our kitchens is cassia. True cinnamon has a much different flavor and appearance: it is very light in color and its bark is very thin and brittle, whereas cassia bark is very thick and hard. True cinnamon has floral and citrus notes and is actually sweet! I always encourage people to try true cinnamon and discover its wonderfulness. You can find it in spice shops or online.

Prep time: 1 hour | Active time: 5 minutes
Serves 4 in 6-ounce glasses

INSTRUCTIONS

1. In a small saucepan over medium heat, warm the milk and sugar. When the milk has just reached a simmer, add the cinnamon and stir.

2. Remove the pan from the heat, and let the milk cool, about 20 minutes.

3. Using a fine mesh strainer (such as a chinoise) over a bowl, squeeze all of the milk from the cinnamon, either with your hands or using the back of a spoon. Discard the solids. (Note: Ground true cinnamon typically has a larger particle size than cassia, which is why it needs to be strained.)

4. Blend the cinnamon-infused milk with the ice cream until they are just combined.

5. Pour into glasses and garnish with a very light dusting of cinnamon.

note
This recipe is delicious as a malt! Just add 2 tablespoons of malt powder to the infused milk and blend well.

boozy shakes

CHOCOLATE ESPRESSO
WHISKEY MALT

SOUTHERN COMFORT SHAKE

SMOKED CHOCOLATE AND
SCOTCH SHAKE

DARK AND STORMY SHAKE

MOJITO SHAKE

COLD BUTTERED RUM SHAKE

THE JOSEPHINE SHAKE

ST-GERMAIN AND
HUCKLEBERRY SHAKE

CHERRY BRANDY SHAKE

PIÑA COLADA SHAKE

WHITE RUSSIAN MALT

CAMPARI SHAKE

CHIPOTLE SPICE SIPPING
CHOCOLATE SHAKE

JALAPEÑO TEQUILA SHAKE

chocolate espresso whiskey malt

INGREDIENTS

¼ cup malt powder

2 tablespoons sugar

1 tablespoon plus 1 teaspoon finely ground espresso

2 tablespoons half-and-half

½ cup whiskey

9 scoops Chocolate Ice Cream (page 18) or store-bought

The first time I ever had whiskey and coffee, I was in Spain volunteering on a farm up in the mountains far from any city. After a couple of months had passed, the lot of us decided to take a trip to the nearest city. It was late, and none of us were used to staying up past 9—coffee and whiskey seemed only logical. And boy is it good! So the Chocolate Espresso Whiskey Malt is an homage to my time in Sella, where many fond memories were created. Jameson is a good whiskey for this shake.

Active time: 10 minutes
Serves 4 in 6-ounce glasses

INSTRUCTIONS

1. Blend the malt powder, sugar, espresso powder, half-and-half, and whiskey until smooth and frothy.

2. Add the ice cream and blend until it is just combined.

3. Pour into glasses and enjoy!

note
I like to use Jameson for this shake, but most whiskey will make a fine shake.

southern comfort shake

This shake is inspired by some of the flavors you might find in the South, such as bourbon, chicory, and brown sugar. You can find chicory root and rye flakes in your health food store or online. Some grocery stores carry chicory in the coffee section. My favorite bourbon to use is Woodford Reserve.

The Rye Crumble makes a great topping for ice cream or a snack by itself. Feel free to double the batch!

Prep time: 30 minutes | Active time: 10 minutes
Serves 4 in 6-ounce glasses

INSTRUCTIONS

1. To make Rye Crumble: Preheat a cast-iron skillet or other heavy sauté pan. Toast the rye flakes over medium heat, stirring frequently until they begin to brown slightly and give off a nutty smell, about 3 minutes. Turn them out onto a plate.

2. Return the skillet back to the stove, and, again over medium heat, add the brown sugar, stirring it continually with a wooden spoon until it has completely melted, about 1 minute. Immediately whisk the butter into the sugar. Once the sugar has absorbed most of the butter, turn off the heat and add the rye flakes and salt. Stir until the flakes are coated evenly with the sugar. Turn the crumble out onto a plate to cool.

3. Once the crumble is cool enough to handle, break it up into small clusters, about the size of a peanut. Allow to cool.

4. To make the shake: Blend the brown sugar, milk powder, bourbon, half-and-half, vanilla, and salt until they are frothy. Add the rye crumble, chicory, and ice cream, and blend until just incorporated.

5. Pour into glasses and enjoy!

INGREDIENTS

RYE CRUMBLE

$\frac{1}{2}$ cup rye flakes

$\frac{1}{4}$ cup brown sugar, packed

2 tablespoons unsalted butter

Pinch of salt

SHAKE

$\frac{1}{2}$ cup brown sugar, packed

$\frac{1}{4}$ cup milk powder

$\frac{1}{4}$ cup bourbon

2 tablespoons half-and-half

2 teaspoons vanilla extract

$\frac{1}{2}$ teaspoon kosher salt

1 tablespoon roasted, ground chicory root

8 scoops Vanilla Ice Cream (page 16) or store-bought

smoked chocolate and scotch shake

I love the flavor of smoked chocolate. As a fourth-generation Washingtonian, I grew accustomed to smoked salmon at a young age, so when I became a chocolatier, I was determined to smoke chocolate. We use smoked chocolate chips a lot in the Hot Cakes kitchen. Scotch was an obvious pairing for smoked chocolate, as it boasts smoky notes that complement the chocolate. My favorite Scotch to use for this shake is Laphroaig 10 Year. If you aren't up for smoking chocolate, you can substitute regular chocolate chips, and the shake will still turn out amazing.

Prep time: 3 hours | Active time: 5 minutes
Serves 4 in 6-ounce glasses

INGREDIENTS

½ cup heavy cream

½ cup Smoked Chocolate Chips (recipe follows)

½ cup Scotch

8 scoops Chocolate Ice Cream (page 18) or store-bought

INSTRUCTIONS

1. In a small saucepan over medium heat, bring the cream to a boil then immediately remove the pan from the heat and stir in the smoked chocolate chips.

2. Stir until the chips are completely melted and the ganache is smooth. Cool in the refrigerator.

3. Once the ganache is completely cool, blend the ganache, Scotch, and ice cream until they are just combined.

4. Pour into glasses and enjoy!

INGREDIENTS

12 cups alder wood chips

8 ounces (1 ½ cups) dark chocolate chips

SMOKED CHOCOLATE CHIPS

Try these chocolate chips in your favorite cookie recipe!

Active time: About 3 hours
Equipment: 3 small foil pans, gas or charcoal grill, large shoe-type box with a tight fitting lid
Makes 8 ounces chocolate chips

1. Divide the wood chips between two of the foil pans.

2. Heat a grill over high heat (about 500°F). Place one of the pans of wood chips on the grilling grate, close the grill lid, and roast the wood chips until they begin to smoke and smolder, stirring them every 10 minutes or so.

3. Meanwhile, place the chocolate chips in the remaining foil pan, and place the pan in the box and close tightly. Place the box on concrete, grass, or another fireproof surface.

4. After 20 minutes to 1 hour, when the wood chips on the grill have blackened and are smoking profusely, quickly transfer the pan to the box alongside the chocolate chips. Close the box and smoke the chocolate chips until the wood stops smoking, about 30 minutes. It's best to keep the lid closed for this entire process.

5. Add the second batch of wood chips to the grill while the chocolate chips smoke. Once smoldering, replace the first pan of wood chips with the second, giving the chocolate chips a second round of smoke.

6. When the wood has stopped smoking, use the chocolate chips immediately or store in an airtight container for up to 6 months.

note

Done by trapping smoking wood chips in a box with chocolate chips, this nifty smoking process doesn't melt the chocolate—just imbues it with rich, smoky flavor. This quick and easy method was adapted from my own lengthy process and a recipe for cold-smoking chocolate in Dishing up Washington *by Jess Thompson.*

dark and stormy shake

The Dark and Stormy has been my favorite cocktail for years. To be authentic, it has to be made with a spicy, premium ginger beer and a fine dark rum with the perfect amount of lime. It is just as lovely paired with ice cream as it is over ice.

Active time: 10 minutes
Serves 4 in 6-ounce glasses

INSTRUCTIONS

1. Blend the sugar, lime juice, ginger, and rum until frothy. Add the ice cream and blend until it is just combined.

2. Pour into glasses and enjoy!

INGREDIENTS

½ cup sugar

2 tablespoons plus 2 teaspoons freshly squeezed lime juice (from about 2 medium limes)

1 tablespoon plus 1 teaspoon finely grated fresh ginger

½ cup plus 2 tablespoons dark rum

10 scoops Vanilla Ice Cream (page 16) or store-bought

tip
Try using Ginger Ice Cream (page 22) instead for spicier version.

mojito shake

Speckled green with fresh mint, this boozy shake is perfect for those hot summer nights. While the traditional drink contains muddled fresh mint, I blend mine right into the shake—I love the texture of the little mint bits bursting with brightness!

Active time: 10 minutes
Serves 4 in 6-ounce glasses

INGREDIENTS

¼ cup plus 2 tablespoons finely chopped fresh mint, plus 4 whole mint leaves, for garnish

¼ cup plus 1 tablespoon sugar

3 tablespoons freshly squeezed lime juice (from about 2 medium limes)

½ cup plus 1 tablespoon light rum

8 scoops Vanilla Ice Cream (page 16) or store-bought

INSTRUCTIONS

1. Blend the mint, sugar, lime juice, and rum until the sugar is mostly dissolved. Add the ice cream and blend until it is just combined.

2. Pour into glasses and garnish with a mint leaf.

note

Depending on where you live, often you can find fresh mint growing like a weed in neighborhoods! In Seattle, where I live, it grows everywhere, making a trip to the grocery store unnecessary.

cold buttered rum shake

Growing up with my brother and sisters, I have fond memories of getting into my mom's tub of hot buttered rum mix and mixing huge spoonfuls into hot water during the holidays. It was one of our favorite treats. So for nostalgia's sake and just the hands-down goodness of the drink, I have included the Cold Buttered Rum Shake in the book.

Prep time: 30 minutes | Active time: 10 minutes
Serves 4 in 6-ounce glasses

INGREDIENTS

$\frac{1}{2}$ stick unsalted butter, at room temperature

$\frac{1}{2}$ cup brown sugar, packed

$\frac{1}{4}$ cup sifted confectioners' sugar

$\frac{1}{2}$ teaspoon vanilla extract

$\frac{1}{2}$ teaspoon nutmeg, plus more for garnish

$\frac{1}{8}$ teaspoon ground cinnamon

$\frac{1}{8}$ teaspoon ground cloves

2 tablespoons half-and-half

3 tablespoons dark rum

8 scoops Vanilla Ice Cream (page 16) or store-bought

INSTRUCTIONS

1. To make the spice mix: In a medium metal bowl, combine the butter, brown sugar, and confectioners' sugar. Using a wooden spoon, stir until smooth and creamy. Add the vanilla, nutmeg, cinnamon, and cloves, and stir until combined thoroughly.

2. To make the buttered rum mix: In a small saucepan over low heat or in the microwave, gently melt $\frac{1}{2}$ cup of the spice mix with the half-and-half. When the sugar is mostly dissolved, stir in the rum, and allow to cool.

3. Blend the cooled buttered rum mix with the ice cream until the ice cream is mostly incorporated.

4. Pour into glasses and garnish with a dash of nutmeg.

note
The leftover buttered rum mix keeps well refrigerated in an airtight container for 1 month. Try it hot! Just add hot water and rum to taste.

the josephine shake

This shake is based on a pastry we make at Hot Cakes, which in turn was inspired by a *financier*, or French tea cake, sold by a local patisserie in the Pike Place Market. My family and I love these pastries so much, I named my version after my little sister, whose nickname is Josephine. The Josephine Shake embodies the cake's wonderful flavor, which comes from a combination of vanilla and almond extracts and dark rum.

Active time: 10 minutes
Serves 4 in 6-ounce glasses

INSTRUCTIONS

1. Blend the sugar, half-and-half, vanilla and almond extracts, and rum well. Add the ice cream and blend until it is just combined.

2. Pour into glasses and enjoy!

INGREDIENTS

$^1\!/_2$ cup sugar

2 tablespoons half-and-half

1 tablespoon plus 1 teaspoon vanilla extract

1 tablespoon almond extract

$^1\!/_2$ cup dark rum

10 scoops Vanilla Ice Cream (page 16) or store-bought

st-germain and huckleberry shake

Huckleberries are a perfect pair with elderberries—both happen to grow in Washington, my home state. St-Germain is made from the flower of the elderberry tree and hails from France. It has a beautiful bouquet of flavor that opens and brightens on your palate upon first taste. One of my favorite liqueurs, it pairs perfectly with huckleberries. Together, they create an exceptional before- or after-dinner drink.

Active time: 10 minutes
Serves 4 in 6-ounce glasses

INSTRUCTIONS

1. Blend the huckleberries and St-Germain until smooth. Add the ice cream and salt, and blend until the ice cream is just incorporated.

2. Pour into glasses and garnish with a twist of orange and a couple of huckleberries.

INGREDIENTS

1 cup huckleberries, fresh or frozen, plus more for garnish

1 cup St-Germain liqueur

4 scoops Vanilla Ice Cream (page 16) or store-bought

Pinch of salt

4 pieces orange zest, 2 inches long, for garnish

note
If you can't track down huckleberries, blueberries are a good substitute.

cherry brandy shake

Cherries and brandy are a classic combo—which makes sense, since brandy is made from wine, and cherry is a note present in many red wines. I urge you to make the recipe for Brandied Cherries (page 116)! They take six weeks to make but are well worth the wait. They make an excellent garnish for this milkshake, as well as cocktails, sundaes, and homemade sodas.

Prep time: 45 minutes | Active time: 5 minutes
Serves 4 in 6-ounce glasses

INGREDIENTS

1 cup fresh or frozen pitted cherries and their juice, roughly chopped

½ cup plus 2 tablespoons sugar

¼ cup plus 2 tablespoons brandy

10 scoops Vanilla Ice Cream (page 16) or store-bought

Brandied Cherries (recipe follows), for garnish (optional)

INSTRUCTIONS

1. In a small saucepan over medium heat, bring the cherries and sugar to a simmer. Stir until the sugar is dissolved. Simmer for about 5 minutes, or until the syrup is thick enough to coat the back of the spoon. Allow the cherries and syrup to cool.

2. Blend the cherries in their syrup, brandy, and ice cream until they are just combined.

3. Pour into glasses and garnish with brandied cherries (or a drizzle of any leftover cherry syrup).

note

Overcooking the syrup can quickly turn it into cherry caramel, resulting in a flavor similar to molasses, so take care not to over-cook. You want the cherry syrup flavor to taste bright, close to that of a fresh cherry.

INGREDIENTS

2 cups sugar

4 cups brandy

2 pounds fresh sweet cherries, pitted

1 cinnamon stick

6 whole cloves

2 whole star anise

1 teaspoon ground nutmeg

BRANDIED CHERRIES

These Brandied Cherries are a must-have for a last-minute cocktail, milkshake, or sundae party!

Makes a 3-quart jar of cherries

INSTRUCTIONS

1. Dissolve the sugar in the brandy in a sterilized jar big enough to hold everything, about 3 quarts. Add the cherries, cinnamon stick, cloves, and star anise.

2. Cover the jar with a tight-fitting lid and refrigerate for 6 to 8 weeks.

3. The cherries will keep, in the brandied liquid, for at least 1 year in the refrigerator.

note
Both the cherries and brandy are delicious on their own and equally as good when served together.

piña colada shake

A virgin piña colada was my favorite beverage to order when eating out with my family as a child. My little sister and I would ask for a side bowl of maraschino cherries to go with it! This tropical classic lends itself well to a milkshake, since melted ice cream is sometimes used in place of coconut cream. The coconut milk powder adds extra flavor and creaminess.

Active time: 10 minutes
Serves 4 in 6-ounce glasses

INSTRUCTIONS

1. Blend the coconut cream, coconut milk powder, sugar, and pineapple juice thoroughly.

2. Add the rum and ice cream and blend until they are just combined.

3. Pour into glasses and garnish with a dollop of lightly whipped cream and a brandied cherry.

INGREDIENTS

½ cup coconut cream

½ cup coconut milk powder

2 tablespoons sugar

¼ cup pineapple juice

¼ cup light rum

8 scoops Vanilla Ice Cream (page 16) or store-bought

1 recipe Lightly Whipped Cream (page 17), for garnish

4 Brandied Cherries (page 116), for garnish (optional)

note
Coconut milk powder can be found at most Asian markets and health food stores.

white russian malt

The White Russian is a creamy, coffee-flavored cocktail that translates perfectly to a malted milkshake. If you don't have any Kahlúa around, you can always just add espresso powder or strong-brewed coffee in its place.

Active time: 10 minutes
Serves 4 in 6-ounce glasses

INSTRUCTIONS

1. Blend the milk and malt powders, half- and-half, sour cream, and sugar well.

2. Add the Kahlúa and blend well. Add the ice cream and blend until it is just incorporated. Stir in the vodka using a spoon.

3. Pour into glasses and garnish with a dollop of lightly whipped cream.

INGREDIENTS

¼ cup milk powder

¼ cup malt powder

¼ cup plus 1 tablespoon half-and-half

1 tablespoon sour cream

2 tablespoons sugar

¼ cup plus 2 tablespoons Kahlúa

8 scoops Vanilla Ice Cream
(page 16) or store-bought

¼ cup plus 2 tablespoons vodka

1 recipe Lightly Whipped Cream
(page 17), for garnish

campari shake

If you like Campari neat, you will like this shake. If you are unfamiliar with the aperitif, I suggest trying some before you invest in this shake as Campari has a bitter flavor not fit for all. Campari is a bittersweet Italian-made aperitif that has been around for more than 150 years. It has a wonderful complex flavor profile, and, like many other bitters, its recipe is a guarded secret, but we do know it is made from a mélange of herbs and fruits. I find it goes wonderfully with grapefruit.

Active time: 10 minutes

Serves 4 in 4-ounce glasses

INGREDIENTS

½ cup Campari

¼ cup sugar

¼ cup honey

Pinch of salt

½ cup grapefruit meat (from 1 large grapefruit)

8 scoops Vanilla Ice Cream (page 16) or store-bought

4 pieces grapefruit zest, 2 inches long, for garnish

INSTRUCTIONS

1. Blend the Campari, sugar, honey, and salt.

2. Add the grapefruit meat and ice cream and blend until just combined.

3. Pour into glasses and garnish with a twist of grapefruit.

tip
This shake is intended to be enjoyed before your meal—who says you can't have dessert first?

chipotle spice sipping chocolate shake

INGREDIENTS

¼ cup cocoa powder

¼ cup sugar

1 teaspoon chipotle chile powder

½ teaspoon ground cinnamon, plus more for garnish

¼ teaspoon ground cloves

¼ teaspoon nutmeg

2 tablespoons half-and-half

½ cup light rum

8 scoops Vanilla Ice Cream (page 16) or store-bought

Lightly Whipped Cream (page 17), for garnish

I developed a recipe for Chipotle Spice Sipping Chocolate at my first pastry chef job. The spicy heat was so edgy at the time, people didn't know what to think of it. When I moved on to Theo Chocolate, the recipe came with me. Since then, spicy chocolate has become so popular, you see it everywhere. The Chipotle Spice Sipping Chocolate Shake differs from the original recipe, but the flavor profile is just as good.

Active time: 10 minutes
Serves 4 in 6-ounce glasses

INSTRUCTIONS

1. Blend the cocoa powder, sugar, chile powder, cinnamon, cloves, nutmeg, half-and-half, and rum until they are smooth and frothy.

2. Add the ice cream and blend until it is just combined.

3. Pour into glasses and garnish with a dollop of whipped cream and a dusting of cinnamon.

note
This shake is hot! If you can't handle the heat, you might want to use a milder chile such as ancho.

jalapeño tequila shake

INGREDIENTS

¼ cup sugar

2 tablespoons plus 1 teaspoon finely chopped jalapeño, no seeds (about 2 medium jalapeños)

2 teaspoons freshly squeezed lime juice

½ cup tequila

10 scoops Vanilla Ice Cream (page 16) or store-bought

4 lime wedges, for garnish

Chunky sea salt, for garnish

Though it sounds unusual, jalapeños work really well in desserts! Their amazing green, grassy, vegetal flavor is enhanced by sugar. When combined with tequila and lime, they make a milkshake that is like none other. For those of you who can't handle the heat, feel free to cut back on the amount of jalapeños. This one's hot!

Active time: 15 minutes
Serves 4 in 6-ounce glasses

INSTRUCTIONS

1. Blend the sugar, jalapeños, lime juice, and tequila for 2 minutes. Using a fine mesh strainer (such as a chinoise) over a bowl, squeeze all of the liquid from the jalapeños, using the back of a spoon. Discard the solids.

2. Blend the jalapeño liquid with the ice cream until they are just combined.

3. Pour into glasses and garnish with a lime wedge and a sprinkle of sea salt.

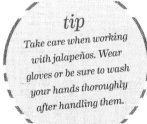

tip
Take care when working with jalapeños. Wear gloves or be sure to wash your hands thoroughly after handling them.

resources

While a lot of the ingredients needed for these recipes can be found locally at your grocer, specialty grocer, health food stores and international markets, sometimes it's nice to use a trusted source. I have listed brands and shops that I have used before, or use regularly. Please consider that because many of these ingredients are seasonal, quality may vary.

Bacon: Skagit River
www.skagitriverranch.com

Butter: Find a local source of organic butter or use Organic Valley. They use local cows for their milk.

Chile Powder: World Spice
www.worldspice.com

Cocoa Powder: Dutched is best for our uses. I like the organic dutched from
www.glorybeefoods.com

Coconut Milk Powder: King Arthur Flour
www.kingarthurflour.com

Dark Brown Sugar: It's very important to use dark! I love Wholesome Sweeteners
www.wholesomesweeteners.com

Dark Chocolate: Theo Chocolate
www.theochocolate.com

Espresso Powder: I love so many roasters, but here are a few of my favorites:
www.tonx.org, www.lighthouseroasters.com, www.bluestarcoffeeroasters.com,
www.stumptowncoffee.com

Flour (Pastry, All Purpose): Shepherds Grain
www.shepherdsgrain.com

Hemp Milk: Tempt
www.livingharvest.com

Huckleberries: Foraged and Found Edibles
www.foragedandfoundedibles.com

Lavender Flowers
www.lavenderwind.com

Malt Powder: GloryBee Foods
www.glorybeefoods.com

Milk Chocolate: Theo Chocolate
www.theochocolate.com

Milk Powder: Organic Valley nonfat
www.organicvalley.coop

Molasses:
www.glorybeefoods.com

Molten Chocolate Cakes: Hot Cakes Confections
www.getyourhotcakes.com

Orange Essential Oil: Dandelion Botanical
www.dandelionbotanical.com

Peaches: Rama Farm
www.ramafarm.com

Rose Water or Rose Hydrosol: Dandelion Botanical
www.dandelionbotanical.com

Rye Flakes:
www.barryfarm.com or your local health food store

Salted Caramel Sauce: Hot Cakes Confections
www.getyourhotcakes.com

Sandwich cookies: Late July organic Vanilla Sandwich cookies
www.latejuly.com

Sugar: Wholesome Sweeteners—organic, low-moisture from
www.glorybeefoods.com or www.wholesomesweeteners.com

True Cinnamon: World Spice
www.worldspice.com

index